THIS IS MY
WOLF CUB SCOUT BOOK

My parents (family) have read the WOLF PARENTS' SUPPLEMENT on pages 4-25 Parents' OK ML

I am Brian Ackerman

I live at 16125 Co. Rd. 6

Plymouth, MN.

Den 8 Pack 283 of

YOU MAY BE A CUB SCOUT, IF:

- You are 8 years of age and not yet 11

or

- You are 7 years of age and have completed the second grade

or

- You have been a Tiger Cub and will be 8 years of age by next December 31.

ISBN 0-8395-3230, No. 3230 • Printed in U.S.A. • 450M585

HERE'S CUB SCOUT FUN!

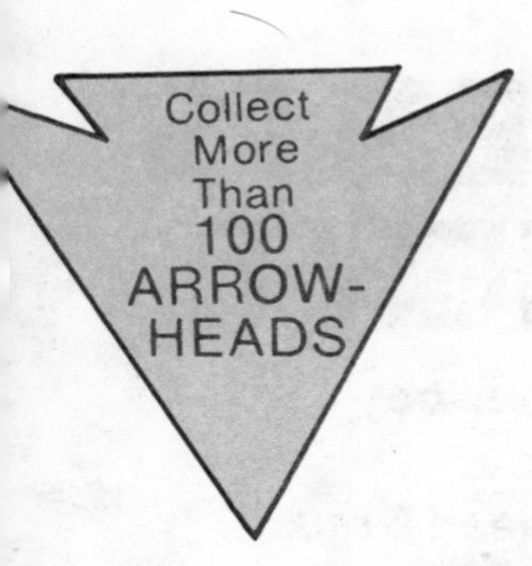
Collect
More
Than
100
ARROW-
HEADS

WOLF PARENTS' SUPPLEMENT

A guide for helping your boy follow the Bobcat, Wolf, and Arrowhead Trails

If you could give your boy the greatest gift of all, what would it be? It wouldn't be money or anything money can buy. Whether you are rich or poor the greatest gift is within your power because that gift is helping a boy become a self-reliant person with a good feeling about himself and a genuine concern for others.

For more than 50 years the Boy Scouts of America has been helping families share this priceless gift with boys.

Baden-Powell, the founder of Scouting, based the Cub Scout program on one of the stories in Rudyard Kipling's *Jungle Books.* It was called "Mowgli's Brothers." We know it as "The Story of Akela and Mowgli." Read the story twice, once to yourself, and the second time to your Cub Scout.

The Story of Akela and Mowgli

Once upon a time . . . in the Seeonee Hills of the jungles of India . . . on a warm summer evening, Father Wolf awoke, stretched his paws and prepared to go hunting. The moon shone into the mouth of the cave where Mother Wolf lay sleeping with their four young cubs.

Suddenly, a shadow crossed the opening of the cave and a whining voice said, "Good Hunting, O Chief of the Wolves, and good luck to your children." It was

Tabaqui, the sneaking little jackal who is too lazy to hunt for himself, so he picks up scraps left by other animals.

Father Wolf told him, "There is no food here, but come in if you wish."

Tabaqui said, "For a poor animal like myself a dry bone is a feast," and in no time at all he was cracking away on a bone at the back of the cave. Now Tabaqui was always ready to make trouble and talk about others. He said, "Shere Khan, the mighty tiger, has changed his hunting ground. He hunts in these hills for the next moon." (Shere Khan was the tiger who lived about twenty miles away, near the big river.)

Father Wolf said, "By the Law of the Jungle, he has no right to change his hunting ground. He will scare the animals away for miles around."

Tabaqui said, "I could have saved myself the trouble of telling you. You can hear him now in the jungle below." And he trotted off to find the tiger.

Father and Mother Wolf listened. They could hear, from the valley below, the angry whine of a tiger who has caught nothing and doesn't care if the whole jungle knows it.

"The fool," said Father Wolf, "to start a night's hunting with all that noise!" The whine changed to a humming-purr . . . which is the noise a tiger makes when he is hunting man. Father Wolf said, "Are there not enough frogs and beetles that he must hunt Man?"

Just then there was a most un-tigerish howl from Shere Khan, and Mother Wolf said, "He has missed! What happened?"

Father Wolf ran out a few paces and looked down to a clearing where there were several wood-cutters' huts. He said, "Shere Khan has had no more sense than to jump at the wood-cutters' fire. He has burned his feet! Tabaqui is with him and they have frightened all the people away."

"Listen," Mother Wolf said, "something is coming up the hill. Get ready!"

Father Wolf crouched and sprang, but as he sprang, he stopped himself in mid-air, because what he saw was a little brown baby!

"Man!" he said. "A man's cub. Look!"

"I have never seen one," Mother Wolf said. "Bring him to me."

Father Wolf brought him into the cave and put him down beside Mother Wolf.

The baby snuggled close to the young wolf cubs. "How little he is," said Mother Wolf.

Suddenly the moonlight was blocked out of the door of the cave by the great head and shoulders of Shere Khan.

"What does Shere Khan want?" said Father Wolf with angry eyes.

"The man-cub!" said Shere Khan. "Give him to me!"

Father Wolf said, "The wolves take orders only from Akela, the head of the wolf pack. The man-cub is ours."

The tiger's roar filled the cave with thunder. "The man-cub is mine. Give him to me!" said Shere Khan.

Mother Wolf sprang up quickly and said, "The man-cub is ours. You have frightened his family away. He shall not be killed. He shall live to run with the pack and hunt with the pack."

Shere Khan knew that he could not fight the two wolves in the cave so, growling and snarling he went away saying, "We will see what the pack has to say about this man-cub."

When the tiger had gone, Father Wolf said, "Shere Khan is right. What will the pack say?" But Mother Wolf had made up her mind to keep him. And they called him Mowgli ("the frog") because his skin was smooth and without hair. So Mowgli stayed with the young cubs.

When they were old enough to run a little, Father and Mother Wolf set off with them one night, through the jungle to a meeting of the wolf pack at the Council Rock. The Law of the Jungle states that the wolves must gather to look over the new wolf cubs of the pack, so they will know them and take care of them when they see them in the jungle.

As each young wolf was pushed into the circle, Akela, the great leader of the wolf pack, sitting high on the Council Rock, called, "Look at each cub, O wolves, look well." At last it was Mowgli's turn and Mother Wolf pushed him into the circle where he sat playing with some stones in the moonlight. Akela did not even twitch an ear as he called, "Look well, O wolves."

From outside the circle came a roar from Shere Khan. "The man-cub is mine. Give him to me." Some of the wolves took up the cry, "What do we want with a man-cub in the pack?"

There is a Law that says if there is an argument as to the right of a cub to join the pack, two people must speak for him. Akela asked, "Who speaks for this cub?"

At first there was no answer, but then Baloo, the sleepy brown bear who teaches the cubs the Law of the Pack, stepped into the circle and said, "I will speak for the man-cub. Let him join the pack and I, myself, will teach him the Law and the ways of the jungle."

"We need another," said Akela. "Who speaks besides Baloo?"

An inky black shadow dropped silently into the circle. It was Bagheera, the black panther, the mighty hunter who teaches the cubs the skills of the jungle. In his soft silky voice he said, "If there is a question as to the right of a cub to join the pack, his life may be bought at a price. Isn't that the Law?"

"Yes," said the pack.

"Then to Baloo's good word, I will add fresh meat which is in the valley below, if you will accept Mowgli into the pack."

The wolves cried, "Let him join. What harm can a man-cub do?" And they came to look him over. Then, one by one, the wolves went down the hill, leaving Mowgli with Father and Mother Wolf, Baloo, and Bagheera at the Council Rock with Akela. Akela said, "Now take him away and teach him the Law of the Pack."

And that is how Mowgli joined the Seeonee Wolf Pack.

After the first reading, find out what Cub Scouting is all about by reading the rest of this Wolf Parents' Supplement.

After the second reading, go on to page 26 and get your Cub Scout started on the Bobcat Trail.

Serious Purpose in a Program That's Fun

While the purpose of Cub Scouting is serious, the program itself is fun because you take the part of the wise Akela and your boy takes the part of Mowgli who must learn from you how to become a resourceful Wolf Cub Scout.

You are one of many adults working with a Cub Scout. As a parent, your responsibility is for one boy. The den leader is Akela for all the boys in the den.

Whether a boy succeeds in the Cub Scout program or quits for lack of interest is up to you! From the time he makes his first promise "To do my best" until he crosses the Webelos bridge to a Boy Scout troop, he needs your guidance, enthusiasm, and active participation in his program.

To help a boy succeed in his Cub Scout activities and advancement program, you don't have to be an expert in Scouting. But you do need to spend time with the boy, learn his concerns and problems, and help him solve them.

Akela's OK

As you thumb through the book, you'll see a constant reference to "Akela's OK." That's you!! A boy can't get credit for any of his requirements until you, Akela, approve them. As you watch a boy

1 Mary Brown 4-7-80 Donna Edwards

BOBCAT TRAIL Akela's OK — Date — Recorded by den leader

complete requirements with your advice and help, you'll soon find you're working together and that's one of the reasons for the entire program—Cub Scout families working together and having fun.

Throughout the *Wolf Cub Scout Book,* special notes for you are printed along with the requirements for special projects which require the supervision and participation of adults. Watch for these "Notes to Akela." They are printed in a smaller type size for your easy identification.

The Bobcat Trail

In Rudyard Kipling's story the black panther, Bagheera, is the mighty hunter who teaches the cubs the skills of the jungle. In Cub Scouting we use the symbol of the Bobcat. You'll find his trail on pages 26 through 35. Along this trail are The Cub Scout Promise, The Law of the Pack, and the Cub Scout motto. These are the three most important things for a boy to learn because they will help him through all of the trails of Scouting.

When you and your boy have followed the seven tracks of the Bobcat your boy may wear his badge.

The Den and the Pack

Cub Scouting is for the whole family and neighborhoods of families. Turn to pages 36 through 45. They will tell you about the den and pack and how you and your boy may fit it.

As a member of a Cub Scout den, a boy meets with his den leaders and fellow Cub Scouts weekly in the home of a parent. In den meetings, the Cub Scouts work on projects, learn games, songs, and tricks to be presented at a monthly pack meeting.

You may be asked to help in one way or another at den meetings, but your main obligation is to attend the monthly pack meetings to see your boy's den and others in action. At the pack meeting held in the meeting place of the organization that operates the pack, you and the boys will take part in a lively program of activities based on a theme of the month.

If possible, the whole family should attend and enjoy the fun and watch the Cub Scouts receive their awards.

Remember! Your boy's success depends on your help, Akela.

The Wolf Trail

The next adventure is the Wolf Trail from pages 46 through 85. This is a big adventure for an 8-year-old boy and the one the Boy Scouts of America hopes all boys will complete. The Bobcat Trail had only seven tracks; the Wolf trail is much longer than the Bobcat's.

When you have OK'd the 50 tracks your boy has filled in, he may become a Wolf Cub Scout. How quickly your boy will become a Wolf is up to him and you. To complete each track he should do his best, that's a part of the promise he made to become a Bobcat (on page 27) and it is the Cub Scout motto "Do Your Best" (on page 33). Don't OK a track if you both know that he can do a better job at this time. Go on to something else, then come back to the problem track. The important thing is to keep him interested.

PROGRESS TOWARD RANKS ON THE WOLF TRAIL. Your boy doesn't have to wait until he completes his entire Wolf Trail before he is recognized for his work. When he completes any three achievements, his den leader can present the Progress Toward Ranks patch to him. It's a square diamond to which a leather thong with a gold bead is attached. Each time he completes three more achievements he will receive another gold bead. With the fourth gold bead, he will receive his Wolf badge at a pack meeting.

As your boy completes the requirements for the achievements on the Wolf Trail, be sure to review his work and sign his book in the place for Akela's OK. At his next den meeting, he should show his book to his den leader who will record his advancement progress and sign the book on the line opposite your OK.

1

Bill Browne — 4/28/80 — Donna Edwards

WOLF TRAIL Akela's OK — Date — Recorded by den leader

The Arrowhead Trail

If your Wolf Cub Scout has not reached his ninth birthday, he can search the Arrowhead Trail. In the Wolf Trail the main sections were called achievements, things that we would like all boys to do. In the Arrowhead Trail the main sections are called electives, choices that a boy can make on his own and with your guidance.

To earn a Gold Arrow Point to wear beneath his Wolf badge he must complete any 10 elective projects of the 106 choices shown in the book. If he does 10 more he qualifies for a Silver Arrow Point to wear beneath the Gold. These are presented after he receives his Wolf badge.

Badges Point the Way

Offering badges is a way to provide recognition, and encourage boys to participate. The Bobcat, Wolf, Gold, and Silver Arrow Point badges are material rewards that mean a great deal to boys who have worked to earn them. In doing these different things, the Boy Scouts of America expects boys to grow in a number of ways.

The following chart may help you see how the purpose is built into the Cub Scout advancement plan. The tracks and arrowheads are numbered in the book and are shown here as they are related to Cub Scouting's purpose. Your hopes for your boy and this purpose may be very much alike. As you read the chart, keep in mind that the plan is flexible. You can adapt it to your needs and situation. It is not necessary to buy special equipment. What is necessary is to be imaginative and make do with what you have.

CUB SCOUT PURPOSE	CUB SCOUT ADVANCEMENT	
Influencing the development of character and encouraging spiritual growth	**BOBCAT TRACKS**	**Page**
	1 Learn and give the Cub Scout Promise.	27
	2 Say the Law of the Pack. Tell what it means.	28-29
	6 Give the Cub Scout motto: "Do Your Best."	33
	WOLF TRACKS (Achievement 11 and part of 12)	
	47 Talk with your folks about their belief in religious activities.	82
	48 Give some ideas how you can show your religious beliefs.	82

CUB SCOUT PURPOSE	CUB SCOUT ADVANCEMENT	
(continued)	**WOLF TRACKS (continued)**	**Page**
Influencing the development of character and encouraging spiritural growth	49 Find out how you can help your church, synagogue, or religious fellowship.	83
	51 Pick a book on a subject you like and read it. Tell a grown-up about it.	84
	ARROWHEADS (Part of Electives 11 and 16)	
	56 Learn the words and sing the first verse of three other songs, hymns, or prayers. Write the verse of one of the songs learned.	134
	76 Talk with your family about what you will do in an emergency.	150
Developing habits and attitudes of good citizenship	**BOBCAT TRACKS**	
	1 Learn and give the Cub Scout Promise.	27
	4 Show the Cub Scout sign. Tell what it means.	31
	5 Show the Cub Scout handshake. Tell what it means.	32
	7 Give the Cub Scout salute. Tell what it means.	34
	WOLF TRACKS (Achievements 2 and 9, and part of 7)	
	9 Give the Pledge of Allegiance to the flag of the United States of America. Tell what it means.	52-53
	10 Lead a flag ceremony in your den.	53
	11 Tell how to respect and take care of the flag. Show three ways to display the flag.	54
	12 With the help of another person fold the flag.	55
	14 Tell three ways to stop the spread of colds.	57

CUB SCOUT PURPOSE	CUB SCOUT ADVANCEMENT	
(continued)	**WOLF TRACKS (continued)**	Page
Developing habits and attitudes of good citizenship	18 Tell how to get to your school, your church or synagogue, and highways or main streets, gas stations, and public telephone nearest your home.	61
	19 Put the telphone numbers of fire, police, doctor, and ambulance at each phone in your home.	61
	20 If you live near some of these, tell how to get to: doctor's office, fire station, police station, bus stop, railroad station, hospital, fire alarm box, post office, airport.	61
	29 Think of six ways to make where you live more beautiful. Talk with your den leader or parents about which one you will do, and then do it.	69
	30 List the ways that you can save water. Tell how you have done one of these.	70
	31 List the ways that you can save energy. Tell what you have done to help.	71
	38 With a grown-up, check your home for things that might cause accidents.	76
	39 Check the outside of your home. Is it clear of things that might start a fire? What about accidents?	77
	40 Practice good rules of street and road safety.	78
	41 Name some things that could cause accidents. Tell what to do about them.	78
	42 Know the rules of bike safety.	79
	ARROWHEADS (Part of Electives 11, 14, and 19)	
	53 Learn and sing the first and last verses of "America."	130

CUB SCOUT PURPOSE	CUB SCOUT ADVANCEMENT	
(continued)	**ARROWHEADS (continued)**	**Page**
	54 Learn and sing the first verse of "The Star-Spangled Banner."	131
	69 Tell what is meant by rabid. Tell what you should do if you see a dog or wild animal that acts as if it may be rabid.	145
	94 Tell some of the fishing laws where you live.	162
Encouraging good sportsmanship and pride in growing strong in mind and body	**WOLF TRACKS** (Achievement 1 and part of 3)	
	1 Play catch with someone 10 steps away. Play until you can throw and catch.	47
	2 Walk a line back and forth. Do it sideways, too, then walk the edge of a board six steps each way.	47
	3 Do a front roll.	48
	4 Do a back roll.	48
	5 Do a falling forward roll.	48
	6 See how high you can jump: OR	49
	7 Do the elephant walk, frog leap, and crab walk; OR	50
	8 Swim as far as you can walk in 15 steps.	51
	13 Show that you know and follow the seven rules of health.	56
	16 Talk with a health-care person about keeping healthy.	59
	ARROWHEADS (Elective 4 and parts of 20)	
	16 Play Pie-tin Washer Toss.	103
	17 Play Marble Sharpshooter.	103
	18 Play the Hat Exchange Game.	104
	19 Play Ring Toss.	105
	20 Play a beanbag toss game.	106

CUB SCOUT PURPOSE	CUB SCOUT ADVANCEMENT	
(continued)	**ARROWHEADS (continued)**	**Page**
Encouraging good sportsmanship and pride in growing strong in mind and body	96 Play a game of tennis, racket ball, or badminton.	164
	102 Show how to make a sprint start in track. Run 45 meters in 11 seconds or less. Do a 1.2 meter standing long jump.	171
	103 Play a game of football.*	172
	104 Play a game of soccer. Show how to dribble and kick.*	173
	105 Play a game of baseball or softball.*	173
	106 Show how to shoot, pass, and dribble a basketball. Take part in a game.*	173
	*If your boy is a member of a team he may get credit for these arrowheads.	
Improving understanding within the family	**WOLF TRACKS** (Part of 4 and all of Achievement 10)	
	17 Talk with others in your home about helping. Agree on the home jobs you will do.	60
	43 Make a game with tin cans, cloth, and beans. Play it with your family.	80
	44 Plan a walk. Go to a park or a woods, or visit a zoo or museum with your family.	81
	45 Read a book or *Boys' Life* magazine with your family. Take turns reading aloud.	81
	46 Decide with Akela what you will watch on TV or listen to on the radio.	81
	ARROWHEADS (Elective 9 and parts of 17 and 18)	
	39-40 Make a gift or toy and give it to someone.	121
	41 Help with a home or den party.	122

CUB SCOUT PURPOSE	CUB SCOUT ADVANCEMENT	
(continued)	**ARROWHEADS (continued)**	**Page**
Improving understanding within the family	79 Fix your own breakfast. Wash and put away the dishes. (It is understood that this is with your permission.)	152
	80 Help fix at least one meal for the family. (Help set the table, cook the food, and wash the dishes.)	152
	83 Help plan and hold a picnic with your family or den.	154
	84 With your folks, help plan and run a family or den outing.	154
Strengthening the ability to get along with other boys and respect other people.	**BOBCAT TRACKS**	
	1 Learn and give the Cub Scout Promise. (Read the explanation for "To help other people.")	27
	2 Say the Law of the Pack. Tell what it means. (Read the explanation for "The Cub Scout gives goodwill.")	28-29
	5 Show the Cub Scout handshake. Tell what it means.	32
	ARROWHEADS (Parts of Electives 2, 3, 4, and 20)	
	6 Help to plan and put on a skit with costumes.	95
	11 Make something useful for your home, church, or school.	99
	16-20 Simple games	103-06
	103-106 Team sports.	172-73

CUB SCOUT PURPOSE	CUB SCOUT ADVANCEMENT

Fostering a sense of personal achievement by developing new interests and skills

WOLF TRACKS
(Achievements 5, 6, most of 7, 8 and 12)

		Page
21	Point out and name eight tools. Do this at home, or go to a hardware store with a grown-up. Tell what each tool does. (If possible, visit places where houses are being built or repaired. Watch the workers use these tools.)	62-63
22	Show how to use pliers.	63
23	Show how to use a hammer.	64
24	Use a screwdriver to drive a screw.	65
25	Make a collection of anything you like. Start with 10 things. Group your collection and name each piece.	66-67
26	Take a hike with your den or your family. Point out things that come from the earth like metal, glass, and oil. Collect three things that can be recycled (used again).	68
27	Go to a store with your den or with a grown-up. Point out three kinds of food. Tell if it comes from above the ground like corn, or below the ground like potatoes.	68
28	List the things that make water and air dirty where you live.	69
30	List the ways that you can save water. Tell how you have done one of these.	70
31	List the ways that you can save energy. Tell what you have done to help.	71
32	Wrap and tie a package so that it is neat and tight.	72
33	Tie a stack of newspapers the right way.	73
34	Tie two cords together with an overhand knot.	73
35	Learn to tie a necktie.	74-75

CUB SCOUT PURPOSE	CUB SCOUT ADVANCEMENT	
(continued)	**WOLF TRACKS (continued)**	**Page**
Fostering a sense of personal achievement by developing new interests and skills	36 Tie your shoelaces with a square bow knot.	74-75
	37 Wrap the end of a rope with tape to keep it from unwinding.	75
	50 Go to a public library with a grown-up. find out how to get your own library card. Name four kinds of books that interest you.	84
	51 Pick a book on a subject you like and read it. Tell a grown-up some things about it.	84
	52 Books are important. Show that you know how to take care of them. Open a new book the right way. Make a paper or plastic cover for it or another book.	85
	ARROWHEADS	
	(Electives 5, 7, 8, 13, and 15 and parts of 1, 3, 6, 10, 11, 12, 14, 17, 18, and 19)	
	1-2 Use a secret code.	88-89
	12 Make a "cm" ruler.	100
	13 Make a bench fork.	101
	14 Make a door stop.	102
	21 Make a model boat with a rubber-band propeller.	107
	22-24 Make or put together some kind of model boat.	108
	26-28 Make and fly a kite.	110-13
	30 Learn to walk on a pair of stilts.	114
	31 Make a pair of puddle jumpers and walk with them.	115
	32 Make a T-stick roller and race with it.	115
	33 Name 10 kinds of trucks, construction machinery, or farm machinery. (Help your boy find opportunities to watch people operate these machines.)	116-17

CUB SCOUT PURPOSE	CUB SCOUT ADVANCEMENT

(continued)

Fostering a sense of personal achievement by developing new interests and skills

ARROWHEADS (continued)

		Page
34	Use a lever.	118
35	Use a pulley.	118
36	Use a wheel and axle.	119
37	Draw a plan for something and build it.	119
38	Make and use a windlass.	120
42	Read a book about Indians.	123
52	Learn 12 word pictures and write a story with them.	128-29
55	Learn the words and sing three Cub Scout songs.	132-33
59	Help draw, paint, or crayon some scenery for a den or pack skit or puppet show.	137
60	Make a stencil pattern.	138
61	Make a poster for a Cub Scout project or pack meeting.	138
62	Make a list of all the birds you saw in a week and tell where you saw them (field, forest, marsh, yard, or park.)	139
63	Put out nesting material (yarn and string) for birds and tell what birds might use it.	140
64	Read a book about birds.	140
65	Point out 10 different kinds of birds (5 may be from pictures).	140
66	Feed wild birds and tell which birds you fed.	141
67	Put out a bird house and tell what birds use it.	142
70	Know what to do when you meet a strange dog.	146
71	Read a book about a pet and tell about it at a den meeting.	146
85	Help plan and lay out a treasure hunt.	155
86	Help plan and lay out an obstacle race.	156
87	Help plan and lay out an adventure trail.	157

CUB SCOUT PURPOSE	CUB SCOUT ADVANCEMENT	
(continued)	**ARROWHEADS (continued)**	**Page**
	89 Point out poison plants that grow near your home. Tell what to do if you accidentally touch one of them.	158
	90 Point out five fish.	159
	91 Rig a pole with the right kind of line. Put on a hook, bobber, and sinker, if you need them. Use it to go fishing.	160
	93 Know the rules of safe fishing.	161
	95 Show how to use a rod and reel.	163
Showing how to be helpful and do one's best	**WOLF TRACKS** (Parts of Achievements 3, 4, and 7)	
	15 Show what to do for a small cut.	58
	17 Talk with others in your home about helping. Agree on the home jobs you will do.	60
	31 List the ways you can save energy. Tell what you have done to help.	71
	ARROWHEADS (Parts of Electives 3, 14, and 16)	
	11 Make something useful for your home, church, or school.	99
	68 Take care of a pet.	143-44
	77 In case of a bad storm or flood, know where you can get safe food and water in your home. Tell how to purify water. Show one way. Know all shut-off places for water, electricity, gas, or oil.	150-51
	78 Make a list of your first aid supplies, or make a first aid kit. Know where the first aid things will be kept.	151

CUB SCOUT PURPOSE	CUB SCOUT ADVANCEMENT	
Providing fun and exciting new things to do	**ARROWHEADS** (Electives 1, 2, 6, and 7 and parts of 10, 17, and 20)	**Page**
	1-5 Secret codes.	88-94
	6-10 Dramatics	95-98
	25-29 Kites	109-13
	30-32 Footpower	114-15
	43 Learn and take part in an Indian dance.	123
	44 Make an Indian tomahawk.	124
	45 Make an Indian spear.	124
	47 Make a set of bell bands to wear on your legs or arms.	125
	48 Make an Indian tom-tom.	126
	49 Make an Indian rattle.	126
	50 Make an Indian shield.	127
	51 Make an Indian costume.	127
	52 Learn 12 (Indian) word pictures and write a story with them.	128-29
	57 Make a freehand sketch.	135
	58 Tell a story in three steps by drawing three cartoons.	136
	81 Cook something you haven't cooked before.	153
	88 Take part in two summertime pack events with your den.	158
	92 Fish with members of your family or a grown-up. Bait your hook and catch a fish.	161
	97 Boating.	165
	98 Archery.	166
	99 Skiing.	167
	100 Ice skating.	168
	101 Roller skating.	169-70

CUB SCOUT PURPOSE	CUB SCOUT ADVANCEMENT	
Preparing them to become Boy Scouts	**BOBCAT TRACK**	**Page**
	3 Tell what Webelos means. **WE'll BE Loyal Scouts** is the meaning of Webelos. To all loyal Scouts there is the possibility of a life-long association with the Boy Scouts of America. The adventure in Scouting is a never-ending trail. When your boy is 9, the Bear Trail leads him on. At 10, the Webelos Trail opens up, and at 11 he can start on his own Trail to Eagle.	30

The Advantages of Scouting

Successful men all over America point to Scouting when asked how they found their life's work. All experiences of Cub Scouting will have an effect upon your boy. Through Scouting he may find his life's work.

Career Education and Cub Scouting

Career education is committed to helping individuals develop a realistic self-concept, with regard to their own needs, values, preferences, and abilities; Cub Scouting shares in these commitments: (1) Career education aims at helping students develop the skills they need to get along with others and to become productive members of society. (2) Career education recognizes the need to have a realistic understanding of the qualities important to personal success.

Through Cub Scouting you can help your boy become aware of career possibilities. This is a natural part of Cub Scouting. Children often like to think about what they will do when they grow up.

Den and pack trips and tours of industry, business, and community installations offer opportunities for boys to see people in action, doing their jobs. They can ask questions, collect information, and soak up ideas for their possible life's work while participating in a program of fun.

You can make the difference in what a boy gets out of a trip, tour, or project. Urge him to ask questions and gather facts. he may meet a person whose job turns him on.

Your boy's understanding of possible career choices and of the world he lives in can be increased starting at home.

Begin helping your boy understand that working both inside and outside the home are important parts of life; and all members of a family can cooperate to keep the household operating, even though parents and children may have additional responsibilities elsewhere. People need to learn to care for themselves and others. A good time to bring this up for discussion is when your boy is working on Achievement 4—Your Home and Community.

Two achievements and 15 electives are related to jobs that people are working at today. Here are just a few examples:

Achievement 11: ministers, missionaries, priests, rabbis

Achievement 12: authors, bookbinders, librarians, reporters

Elective 1: people who teach the deaf, telegraph operators, computer programmers

Elective 2: actors, costume designers, camera operators, sound engineers, producers, stage directors

Elective 3: carpenters, toy and furniture manufacturers

Elective 4: game manufacturers, recreation directors

Elective 5: boat builders, sailors (navy and merchant marine)

Elective 8: engineers, industrial designers, machine operators

Elective 9: hotel managers, caterers, cruise-ship social directors

Elective 12: fine artists, illustrators, technical or advertising artists, draftsmen, architects

Elective 13: wildlife managers, game biologists

Elective 14: zoologists, veterinarians, zoo keepers

Elective 15: biologists, farmers, landscape architects, foresters

Elective 16: police officers, fire fighters, civil defense workers

Elective 17: chefs, nutritionists, food service workers

Elective 18: recreational directors, youth directors, camp directors

Elective 19: fishermen, fisheries managers and workers

FOR MORE INFORMATION

This 32-page *Cub Scout Family Book*, No. 3846, can help you and your family make the best use of your opportunities.

WELCOME TO OUR PACK!

This dark track tells you what to do.

Fill this track in when you have done it.

Learn and give the Cub Scout Promise.

I ..Briana.. promise to do my best
(your name)
To do my duty to God and my country,
To help other people, and
To obey the Law of the Pack

Duty to God means
Put God first. Do what you know God wants you to do.

And my country means
Do what you can for your country. Be proud that you are an American.

To help other people means
Do things for others that would please them.

Obey the Law of the Pack means
Be a good Cub Scout. Be proud that you are one.

When you say you will do something, that is a promise.

When you can say the Promise fill in my track.

1 H Ackerman 10-29-85
BOBCAT TRAIL Akela's OK Date Recorded by den leader

Say the Law of the Pack.
Tell what it means.

The Cub Scout follows Akela (Say Ah-KAY-la.)

Akela is a good leader.

Your mother and father are Akelas.

In the pack your Cubmaster is Akela.

Your den leader is Akela.

At school, your teacher is Akela.

The Cub Scout helps the pack go

Come to all the meetings. Do what you can to help. Think of others in the pack.

The pack helps the Cub Scout grow

You can have fun when you are a part of the pack. Learn things from others. Do things with them.

The Cub Scout gives goodwill

Smile. Be happy. A Cub Scout tries to have a cheerful attitude. Look for things to do for others. They don't have to be big things. Little things help, too.

When you can say the Law of the Pack and tell what it means, fill in my track.

2 K Ackerman 11-5-85 MS 11-6-85

BOBCAT TRAIL Akela's OK Date Recorded by den leader

Tell what Webelos means.

Webelos is a Cub Scout secret.

Cub Scouts write their secrets backwards:

LL'EW EB LAYOL STUOCS

We'll **Be** **Lo**yal **S**couts	**WeBeLoS**

Loyal means that you will keep your Cub Scout promise.

The Webelos Arrow of Light is another secret. It points the THGIR YAW OT OG every day of the week.

When you know what Webelos means, fill in my track.

3 H Ackerman 10-29-85 11-6-85 MS

BOBCAT TRAIL Akela's OK Date Recorded by den leader

Show the Cub Scout sign.
Tell what it means.

Make the sign with your right hand and with your arm held straight up.

The two fingers stand for two parts of the Promise—" to help other people" and "obey." They look like a wolf's ears ready to listen to Akela.

Give the Cub Scout sign when you say the Cub Scout Promise or Law of the Pack.

When you can give the sign and tell what it means, fill the track.

4

H Ackerman 10-29-85 11-6-85 ms

BOBCAT TRAIL Akela's OK — Date — Recorded by den leader

**Show the Cub Scout handshake.
Tell what it means.**

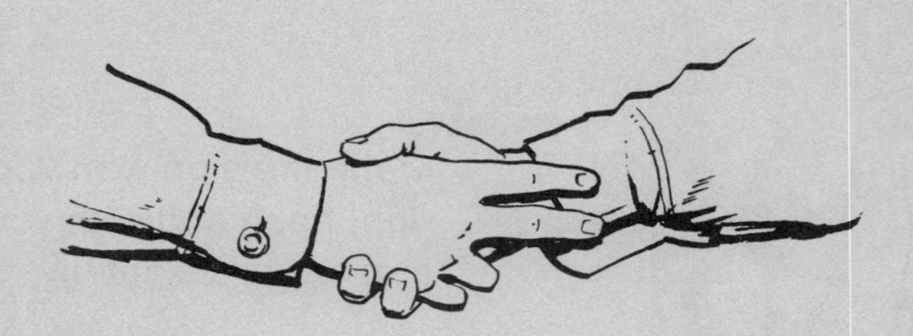

Here's how to shake hands with another Cub Scout. Hold out your right hand just as you always do to shake hands. Put your first two fingers along the inside of the other boy's wrist.

This means that you help and that you obey the Law of the Pack.

When you can shake hands as a Cub Scout, fill in my track.

5 H Ackerman 10-28-85 MS 11-6-85
BOBCAT TRAIL Akela's OK Date Recorded by den leader

Give the Cub Scout motto.
A motto is a rule.

DO YOUR BEST
is the Cub Scout motto.

It means —

When you play a game, do your best to help your team win.

When you study in school, do your best to learn from your teacher.

When you help at home, do your best to help your family. Whatever you do, do your best.

When you know the motto and can tell what it means, fill in my track.

6 H Ackerman 10-29-85 11-6-85 MS
BOBCAT TRAIL Akela's OK Date Recorded by den leader

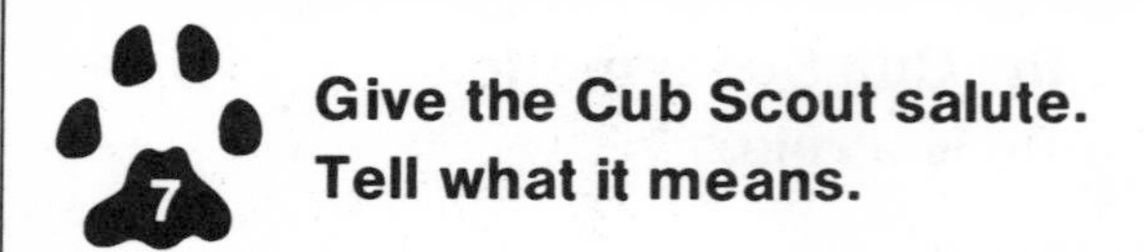

Give the Cub Scout salute.
Tell what it means.

Salute with your right hand. Hold your fingers as you do for the Cub Scout sign. Keep the two straight fingers close together. Touch the tips of those fingers to your cap. If you are not wearing a cap, touch your eyebrow.

A salute is a way to show respect to your leaders. It shows that you look up to them and respect them. We salute the flag to show respect to our country.

When you can give the Cub Scout salute and tell what it means, fill in my track.

H Ackerman	11-5-85	11-6-85 MS
BOBCAT TRAIL Akela's OK	Date	Recorded by den leader

If you have filled
in seven of my tracks,
you have caught me.

Now you are a Bobcat Cub Scout.

Your Cub Scout Den

Bobcats live in dens. So do wolves and bears.

Cub Scouts are like that, too. They meet with other Cub Scouts in a den.

HOME IS WHERE
THE HEART IS

That den is in somebody's home. It may be your own home.

Your den leader may
be your mother, father,
grandmother, or grand-
father; or someone else's.

Whoever it is, that
person is Akela for
your den. Akela wants
every Cub Scout to
have fun and learn
how to do things. You
can, if everyone helps.

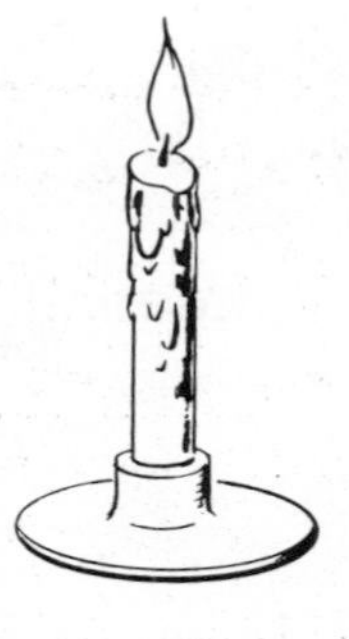

Akela may light a candle
to help you remember to act
your best. When the candle
has burned all the way
down you may be given a treat.

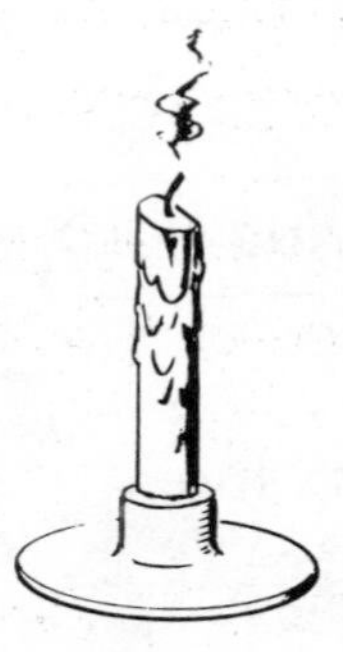

The light will go out if you
misbehave or do not follow
Akela. When the light goes out
it will not be lit again until
the next meeting.

Your Cub Scout Pack

Wolves from many
dens run in packs.
The pack is one
big happy family.

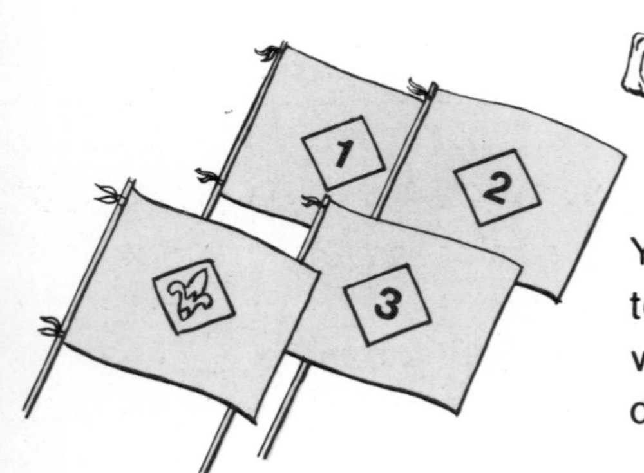

Your den belongs
to a pack. You
will meet other
dens at a pack meeting.

A pack meeting is a show
and each show has a
new idea, like "Cub Scout
Fair" or "Blue and Gold."

Each den takes a part in the show. But pack meetings are not just for Cub Scouts. Pack meetings are for families. They watch while you and other Cub Scouts do your stuff, and get your badges.

Your pack may belong to a church or a school or something like that. Your pack meets there.

The pack leader is called a Cubmaster. The Cubmaster is Akela for the pack.

Den Meetings

What do you do at a den meeting? Lots of things. You better be on time or you will miss something.

When you get there, Cub Scouts may be playing a game or doing a puzzle.

Your den leader is Akela at the den meetings.

Sometimes they will write messages backward. What would you do if you saw this sign?

TIS NWOD

Writing backward is the Cub Scout code.

When all of the Cub Scouts are there,
it is time to start the meeting.

You salute the flag or give the Cub Scout Promise.

Someone will collect dues. Show your den leader, Akela, how far you have tracked the Wolf in your book. Your den leader will mark your book.

Then you will get ready for the next pack meeting.

NEXT
PACK MEETING
THIRD THURSDAY
7:00 PM

Maybe you will play a game that has something to do with the month's show idea. We call it a theme. Or you could do a stunt or skit or make something.

Before the meeting ends you may be a part of the living circle ceremony. Hold out your left hand palm down and thumb out. Hold the thumb of the boy on your left.

DO	**SAY**
Raise the living circle	AH
Lower it	KAY
Raise it	LA
Lower it	WE'LL
Raise it	DO
Lower it	OUR
Raise it	BEST

Or you may end the meeting
with this Cub Scout prayer
in Indian sign language.

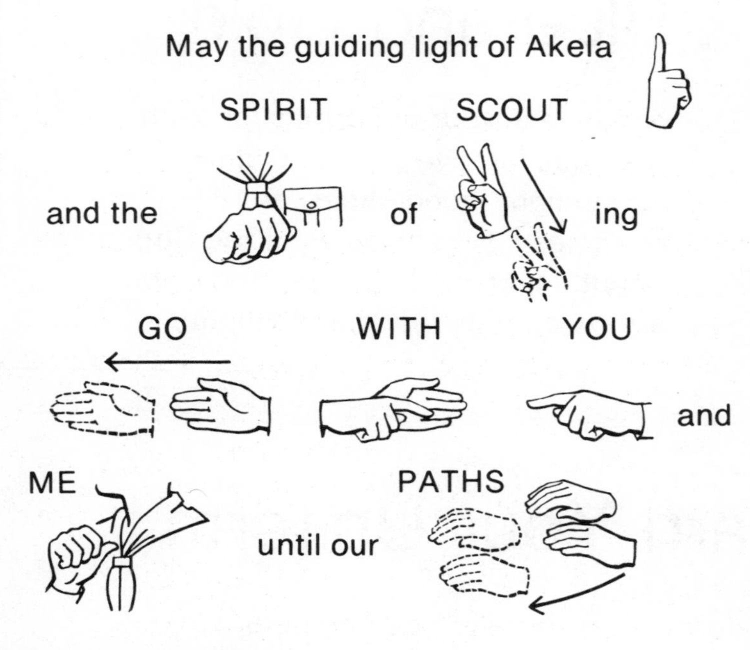

cross again. Amen.

Before you leave do three things:

1. Help clean up the den meeting room.
2. Be sure you have all your things.
3. Thank Akela.

Go home and get ready for more fun.

Blue and Gold

The blue in your uniform is for truth. It stands for love of God. Gold is for sunlight, good cheer, and happiness. When you wear the Cub Scout uniform, people will know you are trying to be good and helpful.

Earn Your Uniform

Uniforms cost money. You can help pay for yours. There are jobs that you can do at home or near where you live. Tell your folks you want to help. Everybody should have jobs to do and you will want to do your share.

Buy Your Uniform

You cannot buy your uniform in just any store. Ask your leader where to buy it. Only Cub Scouts can buy a Cub Scout uniform.
You must show your membership card.

Wear Your Uniform

Wear your uniform to den and pack meetings. Wear it whenever you take part in something Cub Scouts do. Keep your uniform clean and neat. Hang it in a closet or fold it and put it in a drawer or on a shelf.

You can wear your uniform to sell tickets to a Scout show. Don't wear it when you sell something else.

Now, follow my WOLF TRAIL

I'M THE WOLF.

My track is different from the BOBCAT'S. Cats don't show their claws. But wolves and dogs do.

48 TRACKS OF ACHIEVEMENT

1	☒	☒	☒	☒	☒	☒
2	☐	☐	☐	☐		
3	☐	☐	☐	☐		
4	☐	☐	☐	☐		
5	☐	☐	☐	☐		
6	☐					
7	☐	☐	☐	☐	☐	☐
8	☐	☐	☐	☐	☐	☐
9	☐	☐	☐	☐	☐	
10	☐	☐				
11	☐	☐	☐			
12	☐	☐	☐			

Each time you shade in a paw print on the Wolf Trail, check off a box.

This dark track tells you what to do.

Fill this track in when you have done it.

Watch out! Not all the tracks have to be filled in. Sometimes you can choose just one.

ACHIEVEMENT

I Feats of Skill

NOTE for Akela: If a physician certifies that a Cub Scout's physical condition for an indeterminable time won't permit him to do three of these requirements, the Cubmaster and pack committee may authorize substitution of any three arrow point electives.

Play catch with someone 10 steps away. Play until you can throw and catch.

H Ackerman — 10-24-85 — MS

WOLF TRAIL Akela's OK　　Date　　Recorded by den leader

Walk a line back and forth. Do it sideways, too. Then walk the edge of a board six steps each way.

H Ackerman — 10-24-85 — MS

WOLF TRAIL Akela's OK　　Date　　Recorded by den leader

Do a front roll.

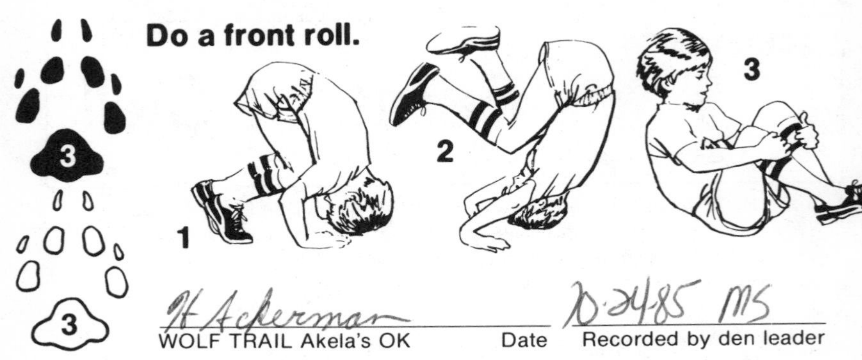

H Ackerman ______ 10·24·85 MS

WOLF TRAIL Akela's OK Date Recorded by den leader

Do a back roll.

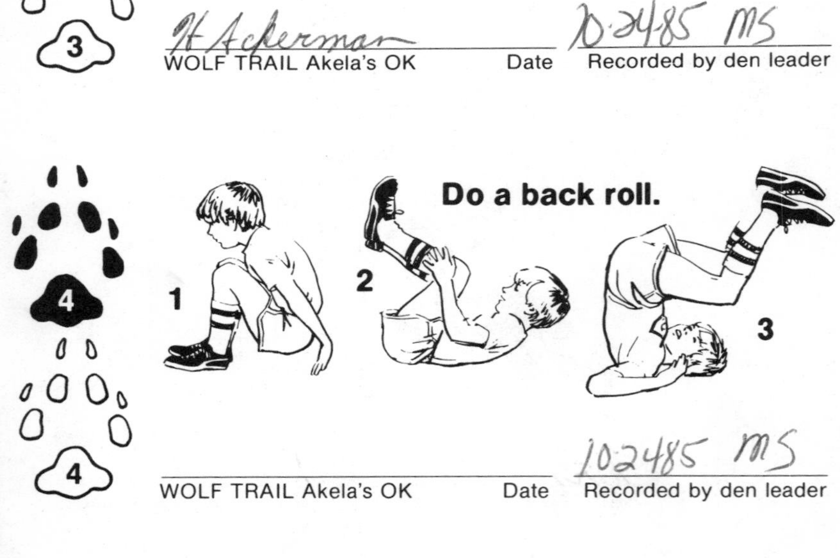

______ 10·24·85 MS

WOLF TRAIL Akela's OK Date Recorded by den leader

Do a falling forward roll.

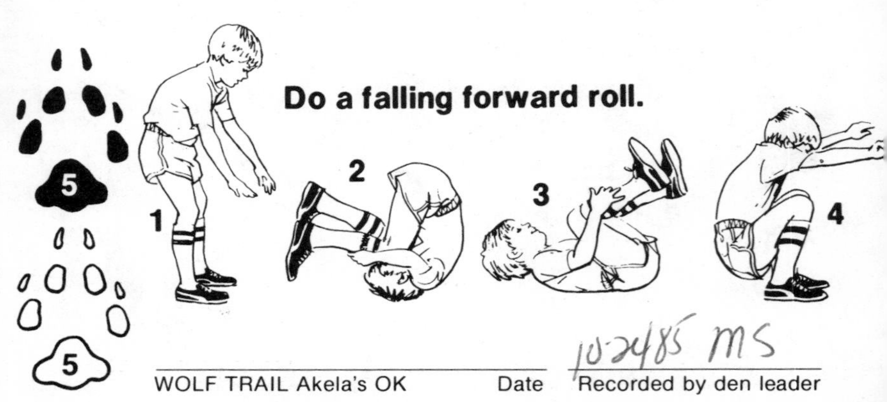

______ 10·24·85 MS

WOLF TRAIL Akela's OK Date Recorded by den leader

DO THIS

See how high you can jump.

Count down from 10 to 0
and coil your body for a blast-off.

When you come to 0, yell blast-off
and jump as high into the air as you can.
Land on your feet.

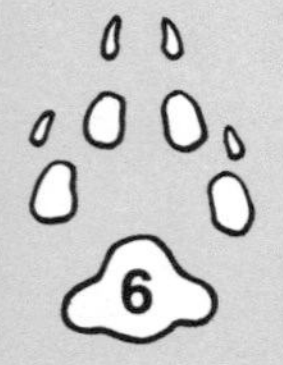

10-24-85 ms

WOLF TRAIL Akela's OK ______ Date ______ Recorded by den leader

OR THIS

Do the elephant walk, frog leap, and crab walk.

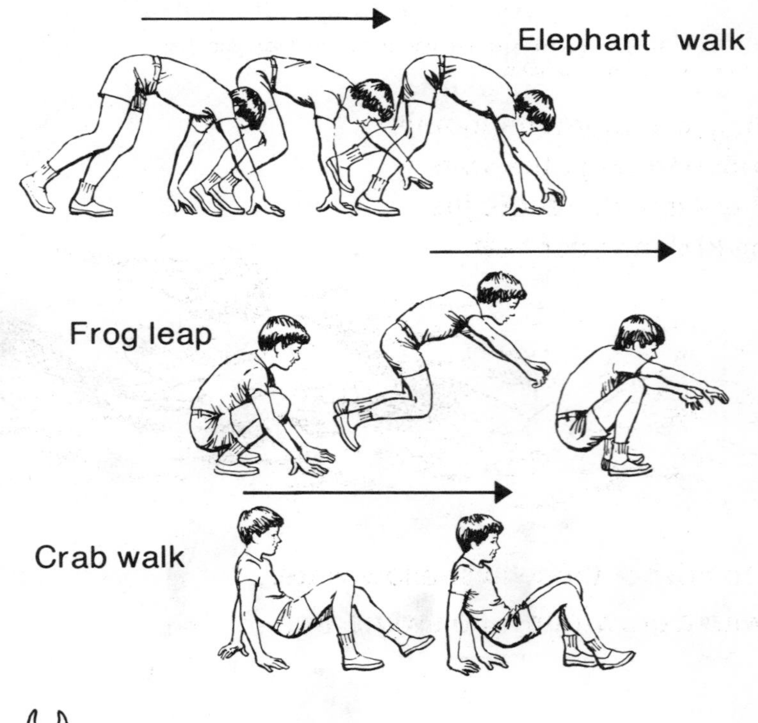

WOLF TRAIL Akela's OK ______ Date ______ Recorded by den leader ______

Swim as far as you can walk in 15 steps.

NOTE for Akela: Measure at the side of the pool, or along the shore of a pond, or lake.

Hold onto something and move through the water the same distance, just by kicking your feet.

Do both of these in shallow water, with a grown-up who swims well.

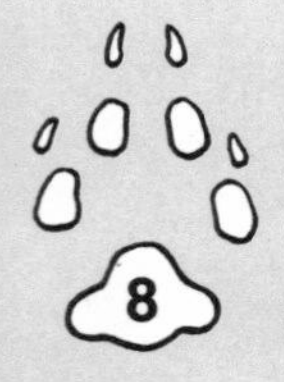

WOLF TRAIL Akela's OK ______ Date ______ Recorded by den leader

ACHIEVEMENT

2 Flag

Give the Pledge of Allegiance to the flag of the United States of America. Tell what it means.

I pledge allegiance
to the flag of the
United States of America
and to the Republic
for which it stands,
one Nation under God,
indivisible,
with liberty and justice for all.

A **pledge** is a promise.
Allegiance is to be true.
Republic is our kind of government.
Nation is our country.
God is the one we worship.
Indivisible is one that cannot be divided into pieces or parts.
Liberty is freedom for you and for others.
Justice is what is right.

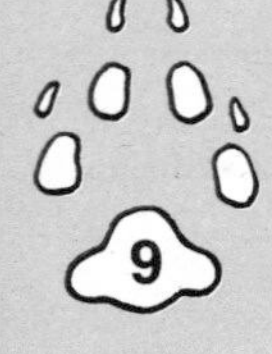

WOLF TRAIL Akela's OK | Date | Recorded by den leader

Lead a flag ceremony in your den. Here are some ideas:

Get your den to stand in a straight line and face the flag. Salute and give the Pledge of Allegiance.

OR

Stand in a square. Bring in the flag. Salute and give the Cub Scout Promise.

OR

Stand in a circle around the flag. Salute and give the Pledge of Allegiance.

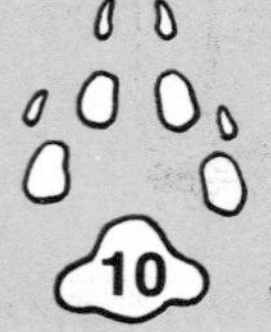

WOLF TRAIL Akela's OK | Date | Recorded by den leader

Tell how to respect and take care of the flag. Show three ways to display the flag.

Here are three secrets:

1. OD TON TEL EHT GALF TEG YTRID.

2. OD TON TEL EHT GALF TEG NROT.

3. OD TON TEL EHT GALF HCUOT EHT DNUORG.

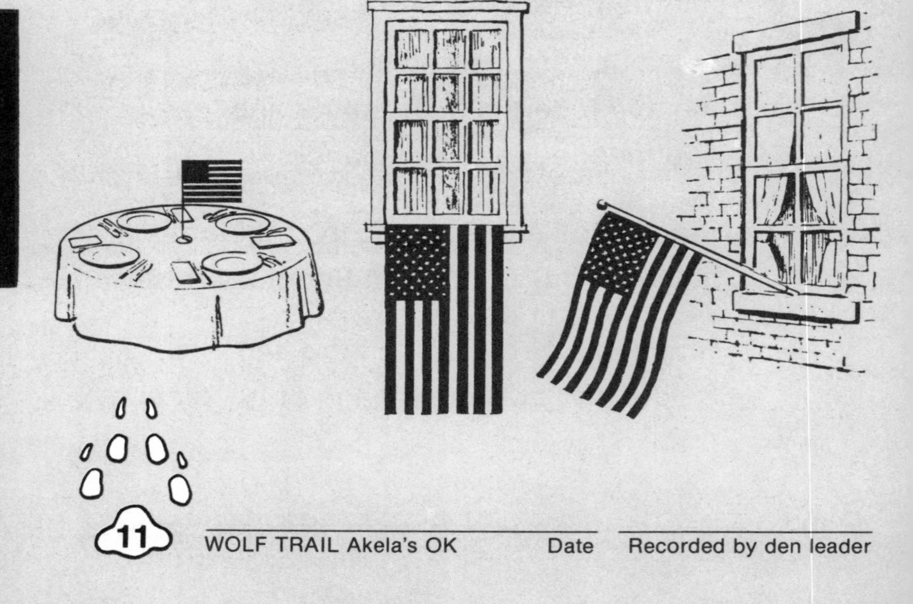

With the help of another person fold the flag.

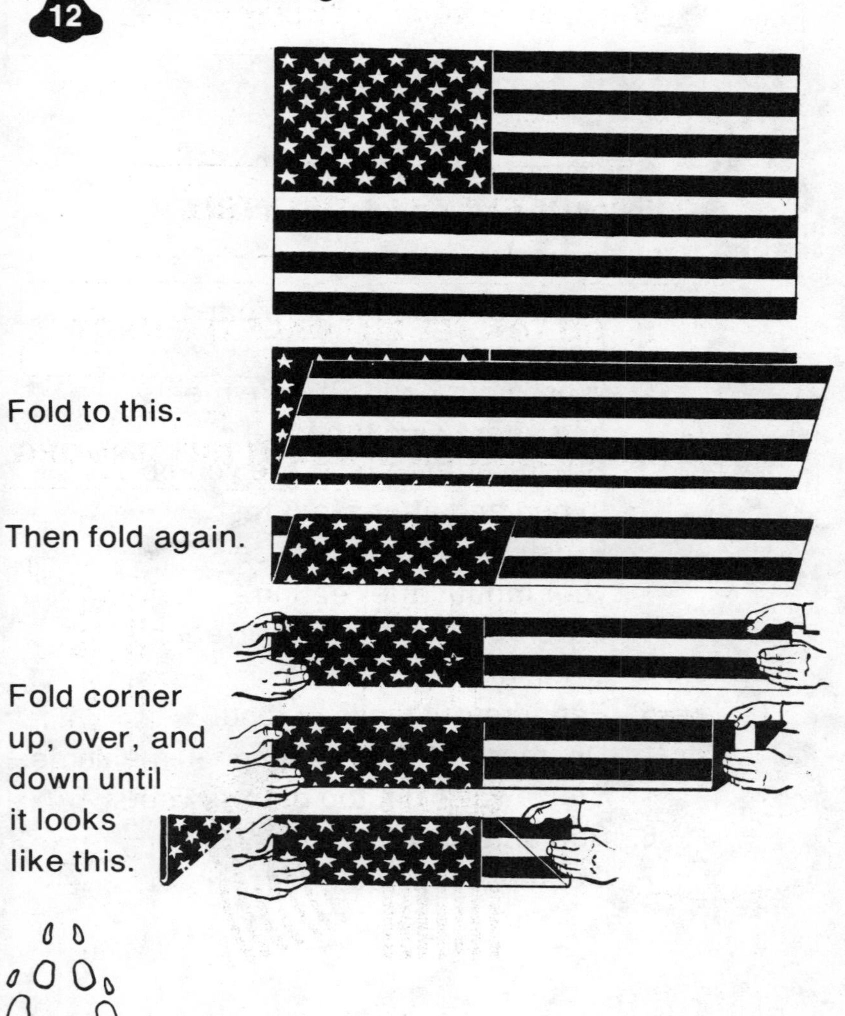

Fold to this.

Then fold again.

Fold corner up, over, and down until it looks like this.

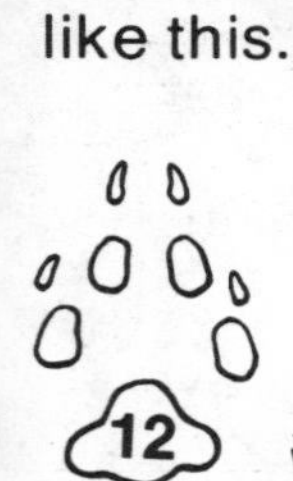

WOLF TRAIL Akela's OK ______ Date ______ Recorded by den leader

ACHIEVEMENT

3 Keeping Healthy

Show that you know and follow the seven rules of health.

1. Take baths or showers often. Use soap.
2. Wash your hands before meals and after using the toilet.
3. Brush your teeth before you go to bed and after breakfast. Brush your teeth or rinse your mouth after eating. See your dentist twice a year.
4. Drink lots of water.
5. Eat different kinds of food. Do most of your eating at mealtime. Stay away from too many sweets.
6. Run and play outdoors.
7. Get the sleep you need.

WOLF TRAIL Akela's OK ______ Date ______ Recorded by den leader ______

Tell three ways to stop the spread of colds.

1. If you have a cold, stay away from other people.

2. Get lots of rest.

3. Turn your head away from others when you sneeze or cough. Cover your mouth and nose.

WOLF TRAIL Akela's OK ______ Date ______ Recorded by den leader

Show what to do for a small cut.

1. Tell a grown-up about the cut.

2. Let the cut bleed a little.

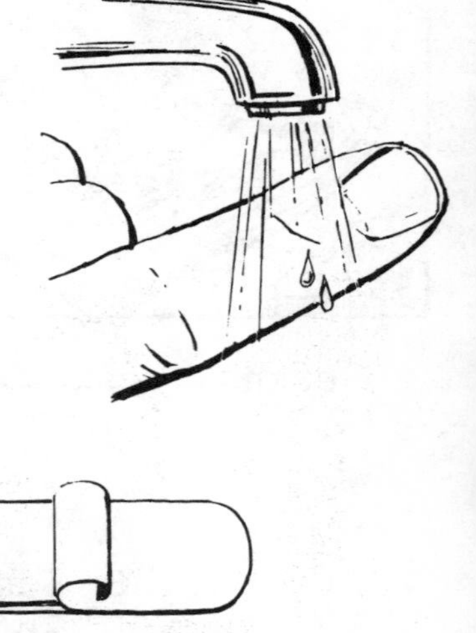

3. Wash it with soap and water.

4. Cover it with a stick-on bandage.

For a big cut, get help fast.

WOLF TRAIL Akela's OK ____________ Date ____________ Recorded by den leader ____________

Talk with a health-care person about keeping healthy.

NOTE to Akela: This can be a doctor, dentist, eye doctor, nurse, first aid member, etc.

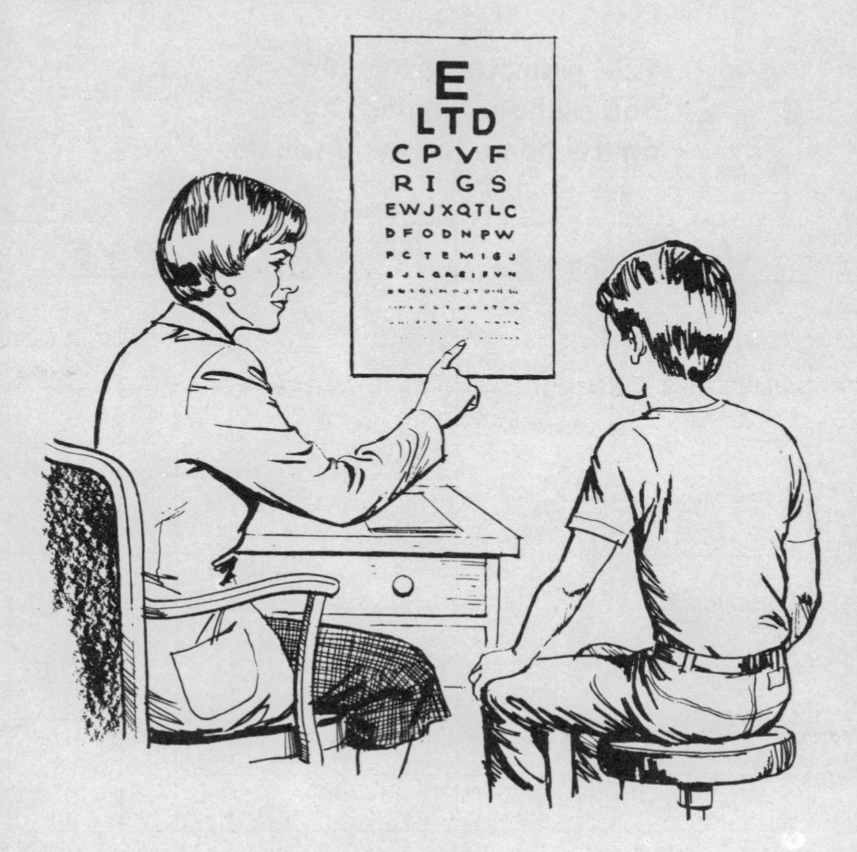

WOLF TRAIL Akela's OK	Date	Recorded by den leader

ACHIEVEMENT

4 Your Home and Community

Talk with others in your home about helping. Agree on the home jobs you will do.

JOB	WHEN	DONE			

WOLF TRAIL Akela's OK ______ Date ______ Recorded by den leader ______

Tell how to get to your school, your church or synagogue, and highways or main streets, gas stations, and public telephone nearest your home.

WOLF TRAIL Akela's OK | Date | Recorded by den leader

Put the telephone numbers of fire, police, doctor, and ambulance at each phone in your home.

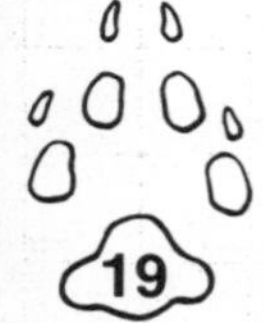

WOLF TRAIL Akela's OK | Date | Recorded by den leader

If you live near some of these, tell how to get to:

Doctor's office
Fire station
Police station
Bus stop
Railroad station
Hospital
Fire alarm box
Post office
Airport

WOLF TRAIL Akela's OK | Date | Recorded by den leader

ACHIEVEMENT

5 Tools

Point out and name eight tools. Do this at home, or go to a hardware store with a grown-up. Tell what each tool does.

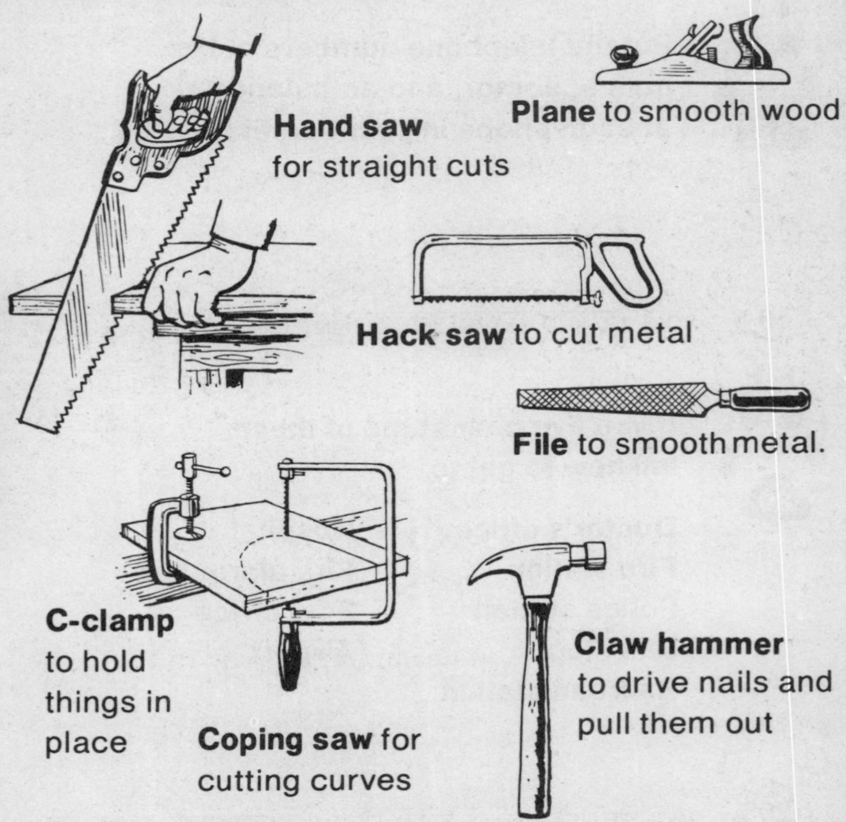

Awl to punch holes.

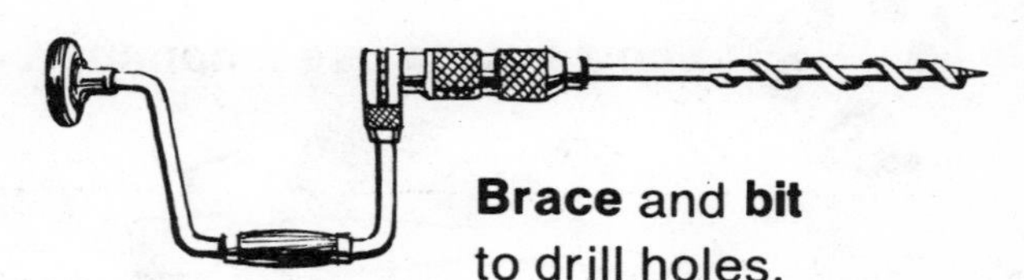

Brace and **bit** to drill holes.

WOLF TRAIL Akela's OK Date Recorded by den leader

Show how to use pliers.

Slip-joint pliers

Slip joint is like this for small jobs.

Slip the joint this way for big jobs.

WOLF TRAIL Akela's OK Date Recorded by den leader

Show how to use a hammer.

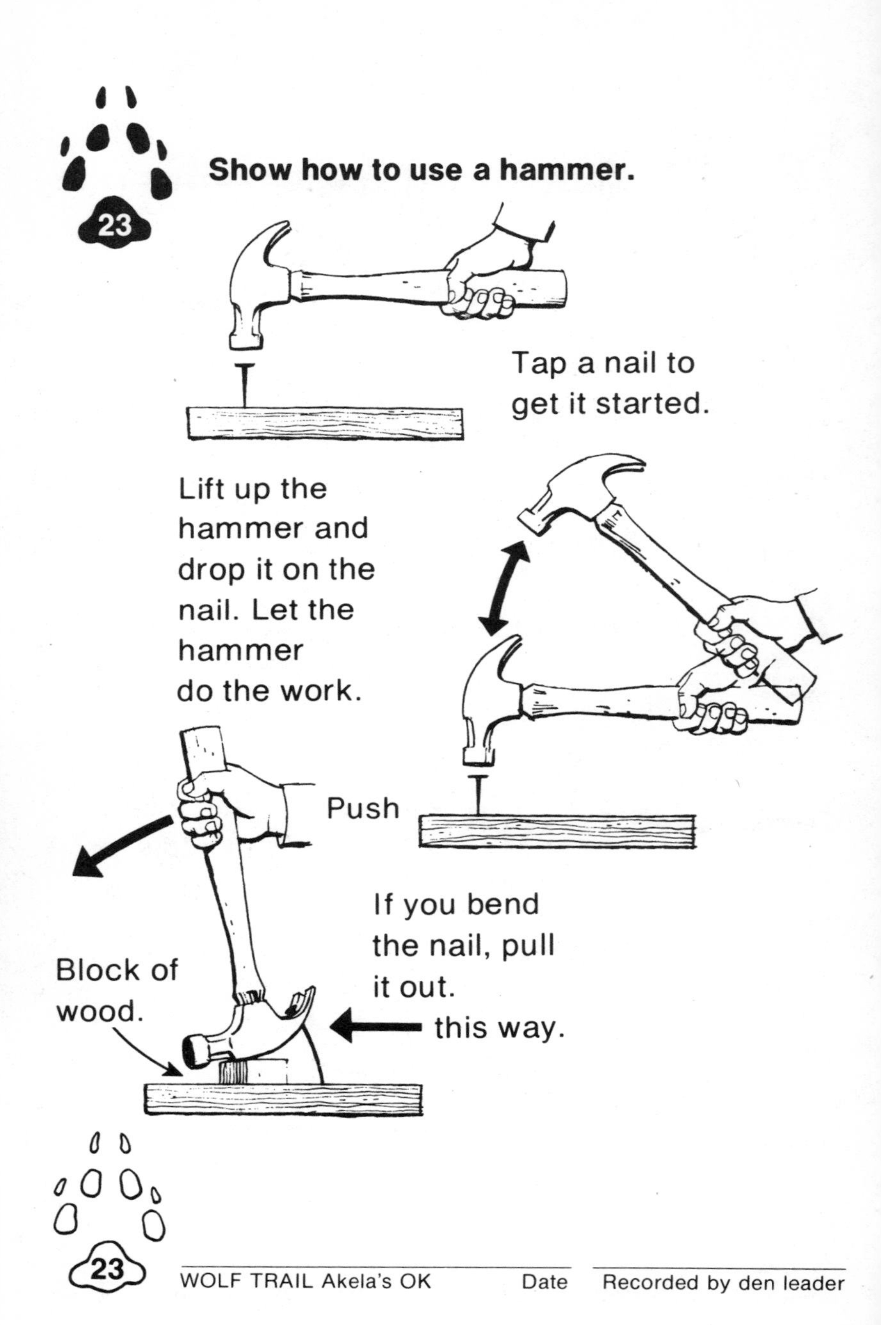

WOLF TRAIL Akela's OK ______ Date ______ Recorded by den leader ______

Use a screwdriver to drive a screw.

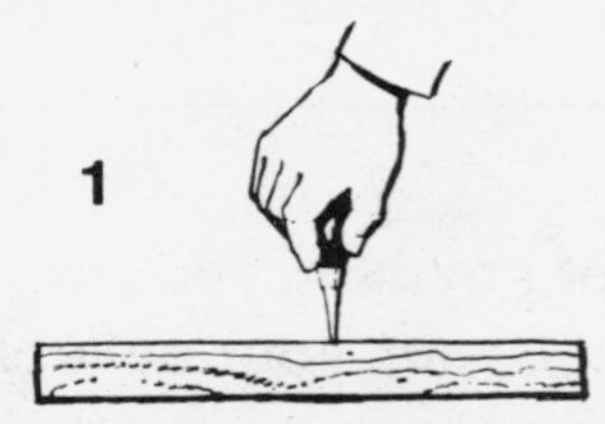

Start a hole in the wood with an awl or a nail.

A screw with soap on it is easier to turn.

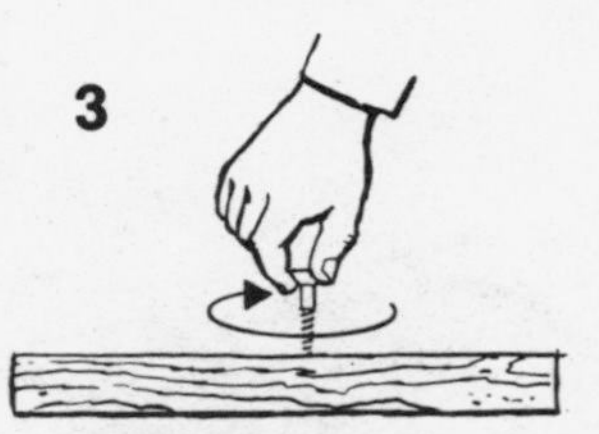

Twist the screw into the hole.

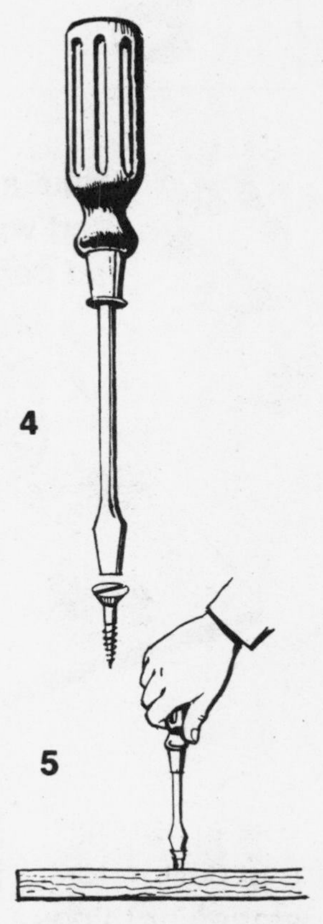

Turn the screw until the head is in the wood.

WOLF TRAIL Akela's OK ____________ Date ____________ Recorded by den leader

ACHIEVEMENT

6 Collections

Make a collection of anything you like. Start with 10 things. Group your collection and name each piece.

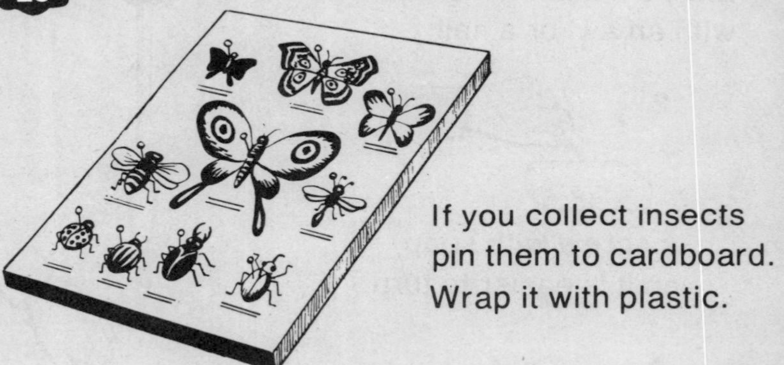

If you collect insects pin them to cardboard. Wrap it with plastic.

Use an empty egg carton for stones or things like that.

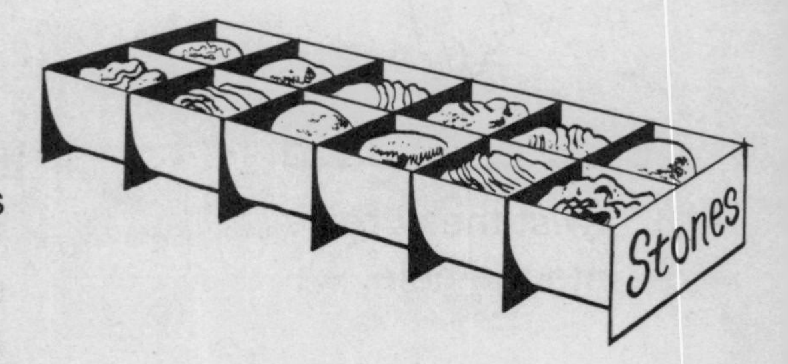

Hold shells in place with wire or glue.

Use stamp hinges to put stamps in a book.

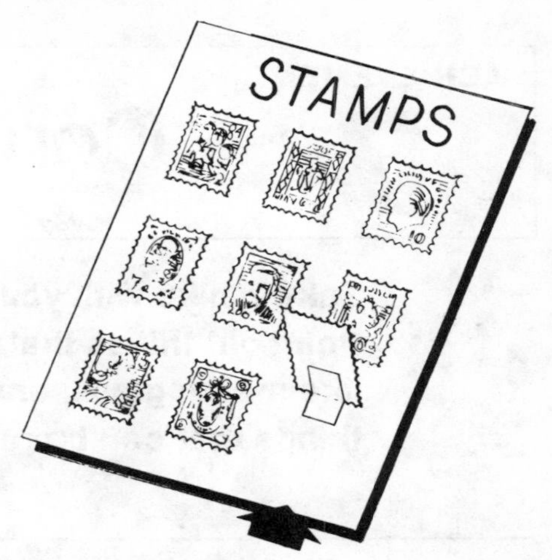

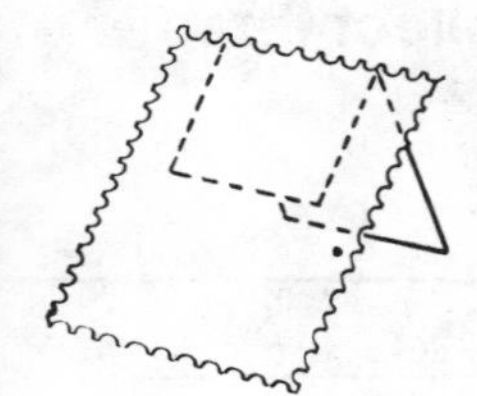

Paste the stamp hinge to the back of the stamp. Then fold it down.

I made a collection of ______________________________

____

____

I showed it and explained it to ______________________________

____

____

______________________ WOLF TRAIL Akela's OK   Date   ______________________ Recorded by den leader

ACHIEVEMENT

7 Conservation

Take a hike with your den or your family. Point out things that come from the earth like metal, glass, and oil. Collect three things that can be recycled.

____

____

____

WOLF TRAIL Akela's OK ______ Date ______ Recorded by den leader ______

Go to a store with your den or with a grown-up. Point out three kinds of food. Tell if it comes from above the ground like corn, or below the ground like potatoes.

____

____

____

WOLF TRAIL Akela's OK ______ Date ______ Recorded by den leader ______

List the things that make water and air dirty where you live.

____

____

____

28

WOLF TRAIL Akela's OK | Date | Recorded by den leader

29

Think of six ways to make where you live more beautiful. Talk with your den leader or parents about which one you will do, and then do it.

1. ____
2. ____
3. ____
4. ____
5. ____
6. ____

Everyone should pick up papers.

29

WOLF TRAIL Akela's OK | Date | Recorded by den leader

List the ways that you can save water.
Tell how you have done one of these.

Don't let the water run to cool it. Put a bottle of drinking water in the refrigerator.

My ideas ____

____

____

____

I have ____

____

____

WOLF TRAIL Akela's OK	Date	Recorded by den leader

List the ways that you can save energy. Tell what you have done to help.

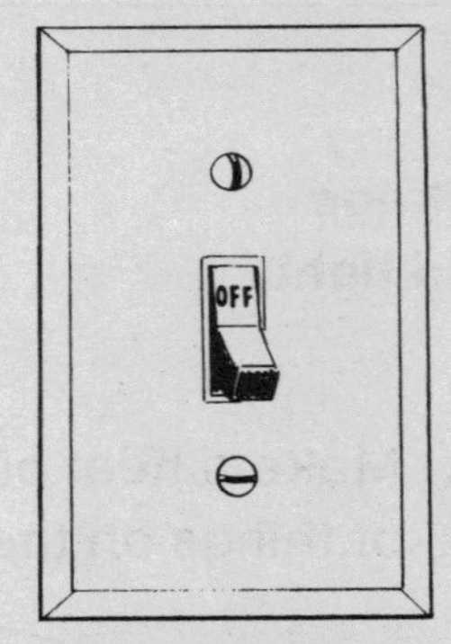

Turn lights off.

Keep refrigerator door closed.

My ideas ____

____

____

____

I helped ____

____

____

WOLF TRAIL Akela's OK ______ Date ______ Recorded by den leader ______

ACHIEVEMENT

8 Tying Things

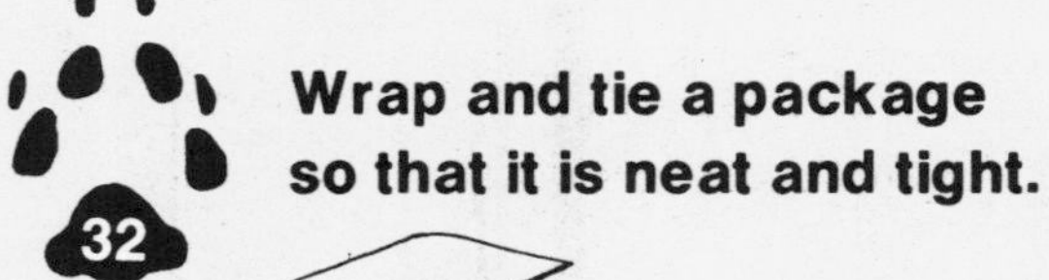

Wrap and tie a package so that it is neat and tight.

1. Make a neat pile of things on the paper.

2. Fold over the long sides of the paper Fold in the ends.

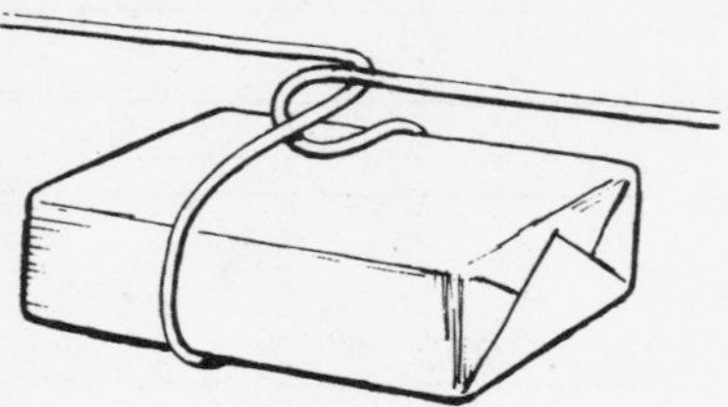

3. Go once around and cross over the string.

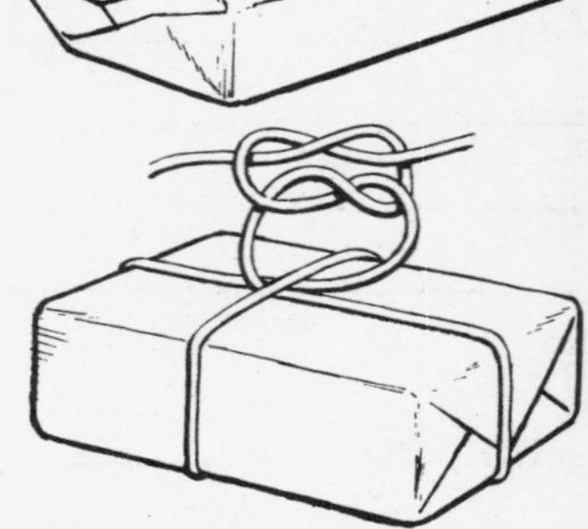

4. Flip over and tie with a square knot.

WOLF TRAIL Akela's OK ______ Date ______ Recorded by den leader ______

Tie a stack of newspapers the right way.

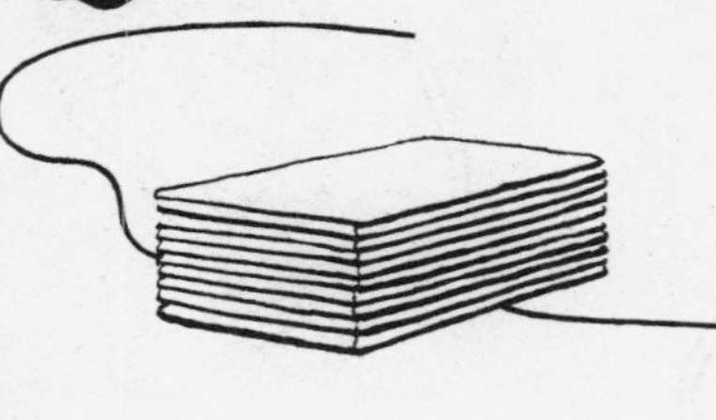

Pile the newspapers on a piece of string. Then tie it like a package.

WOLF TRAIL Akela's OK Date Recorded by den leader

Tie two cords together with an overhand knot.

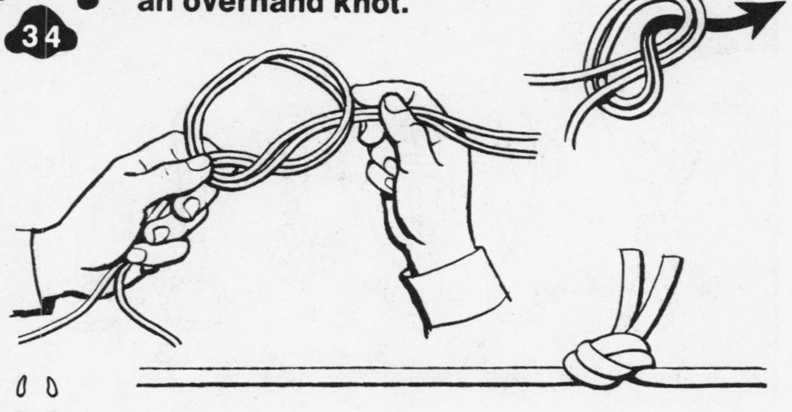

WOLF TRAIL Akela's OK Date Recorded by den leader

Tie your shoelaces with a square bow knot.

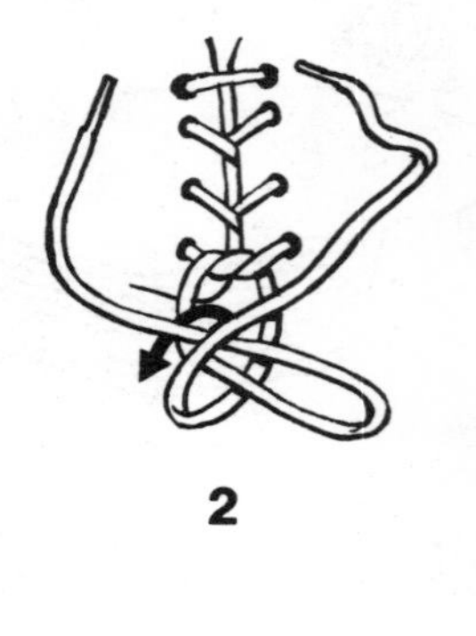

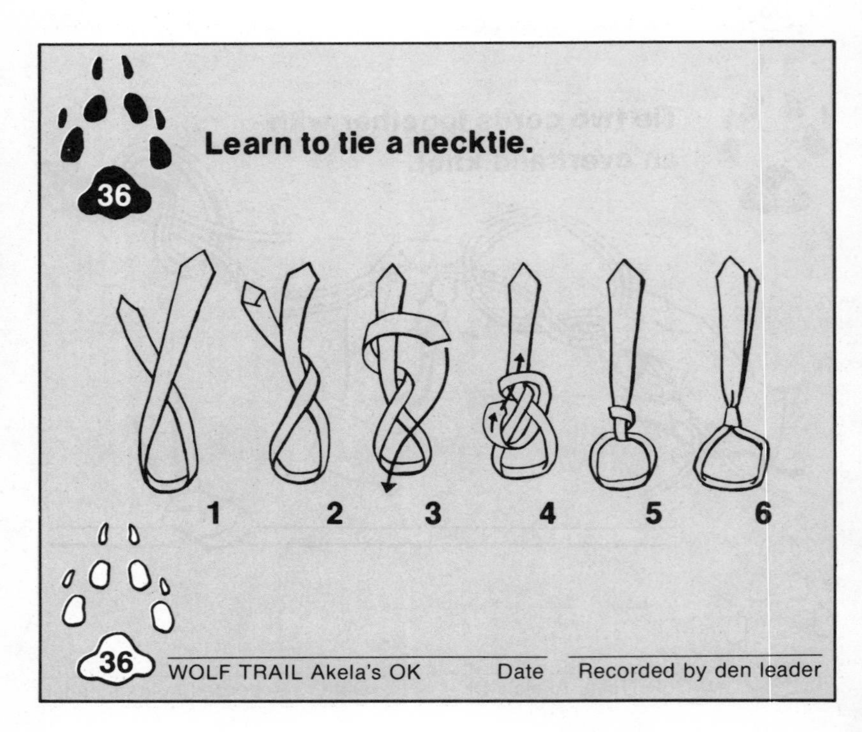

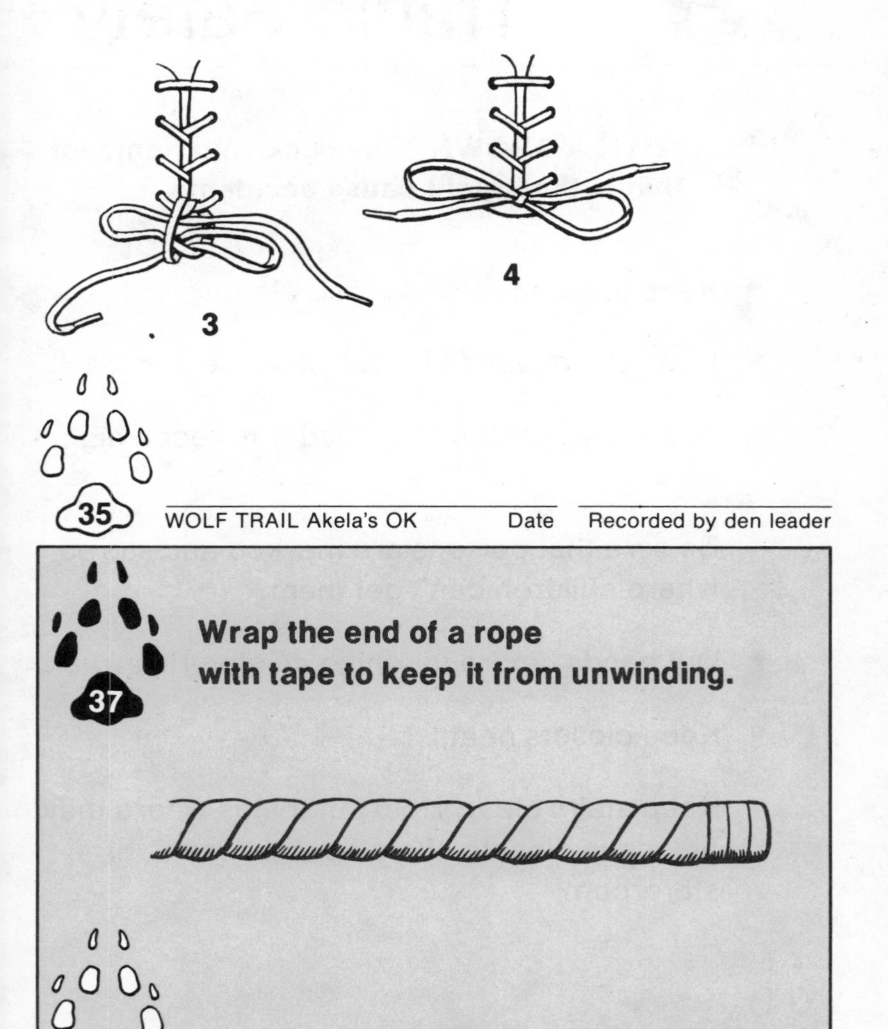

35 WOLF TRAIL Akela's OK Date Recorded by den leader

37

Wrap the end of a rope with tape to keep it from unwinding.

37 WOLF TRAIL Akela's OK Date Recorded by den leader

ACHIEVEMENT 9 Home and Traffic Safety

WITH A GROWN-UP, check your home for things that might cause accidents.

- Keep tools and toys in their places.
- Keep storage areas clear of waste and trash.
- Use a step stool or stepladder to reach high places
- Be sure that poisons are marked and stored where children can't get them.
- Dry hands before touching an electric switch.
- Keep closets neat.
- Keep stairs clear. Help put things where they belong in closets, the attic, basement, or storeroom.

WOLF TRAIL Akela's OK ____ Date ____ Recorded by den leader

Check the outside of your home. Is it clear of things that might start a fire? What about accidents?

- Don't play with matches.
- Ask a grown-up to keep gasoline and other dangerous things marked and away from fires or strong heat.
- Keep matches where small children cannot reach them.
- Keep sidewalks and driveways clear.
- Know where the fire exits are in all the buildings you enter. Look for EXIT signs.
- Tell your family about what you found.

WOLF TRAIL Akela's OK ________ Date ________ Recorded by den leader

Practice good rules of street and road safety.

- Don't play in the street.
- Walk on the left side of the road when there is no sidewalk. Face traffic, watch out for cars.
- Obey traffic signs.
- Cross at crossings. Watch traffic and look both ways before you step into the street.
- Fasten your seat belt every time you ride in a car.

WOLF TRAIL Akela's OK ______ Date ______ Recorded by den leader

Name some things that could cause highway accidents. Tell what to do about them.

WOLF TRAIL Akela's OK ______ Date ______ Recorded by den leader

Know the rules of bike safety.

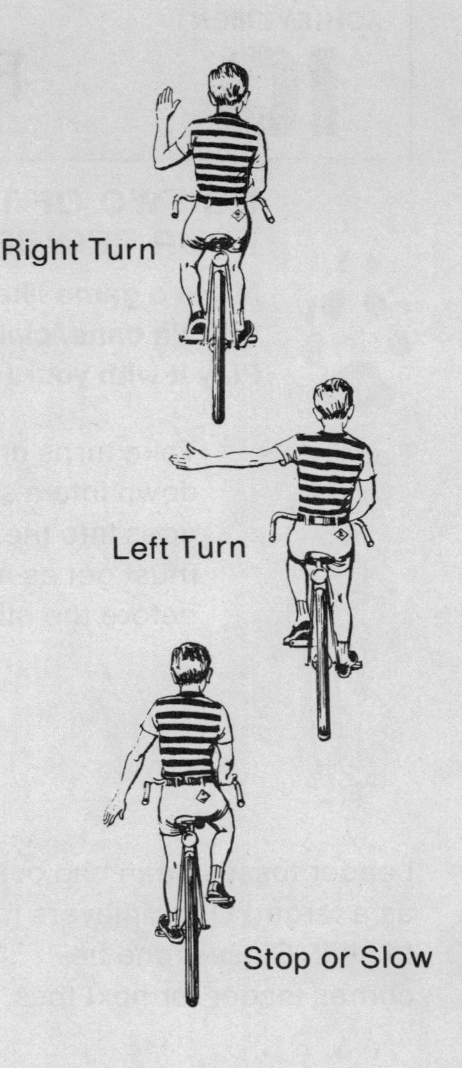

- Ride your bike in a safe place.
- Watch out for others.
- If you have to ride in the road, keep to the right.
- With your left arm, show others what you are going to do.
- Watch out for drain grates.
- Don't be a show-off.

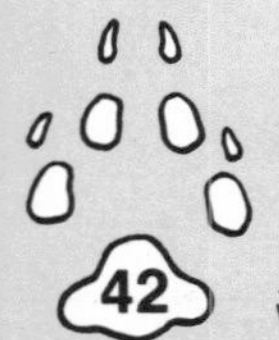

WOLF TRAIL Akela's OK ________ Date ________ Recorded by den leader ________

ACHIEVEMENT

10 Family Fun

DO TWO OF THESE FOUR REQUIREMENTS

Make a game like one of these with tin cans, cloth, and beans. Play it with your family.

Eagle Golf

Take turns dropping something straight down into a small tin can. Each time it goes into the can is 1 point. To win you must get as many points as you are old before the other players.

Bean Bag Archery

Bull's–eye

Leader tosses bean bag out as a target. Other players try to hit it. Closest one becomes leader for next toss.

WOLF TRAIL Akela's OK ______ Date ______ Recorded by den leader ______

Plan a walk. Go to a park or a woods, or visit a zoo or museum with your family.

We went to ______________________________

____

44 ______________ ______________ ______________

WOLF TRAIL Akela's OK Date Recorded by den leader

45 **Read a book or *Boys' Life* magazine with your family. Take turns reading aloud.**

We read ______________________________

____

45 ______________ ______________ ______________

WOLF TRAIL Akela's OK Date Recorded by den leader

46 **Decide with Akela what you will watch on TV or listen to on the radio.**

46 ______________ ______________ ______________

WOLF TRAIL Akela's OK Date Recorded by den leader

ACHIEVEMENT

Religious Activities

Cub Scout Promise

I .... promise to do my best
(your name)
To do my duty to God and my country,
To help other people, and
To obey the Law of the Pack

Talk with your folks about their belief in religious activities.

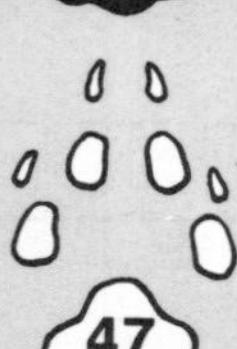

WOLF TRAIL Akela's OK  Date Recorded by den leader

Give some ideas how you can show your religious beliefs.

____

____

____

WOLF TRAIL Akela's OK Date Recorded by den leader

Find out how you can help your church, synagogue, or religious fellowship.

NOTE for Akela: Ask your religious leader or council service center about the religious emblems programs available to Cub Scouts.

I found out that ____________

____

____

____

____

____

____

____

____

Aleph
Jewish

God and Family
Lutheran

God and Country
Episcopal Protestant
(God and Me for 8-year-olds
God and Family for 9- and 10-year-olds)

Metta
Buddhist

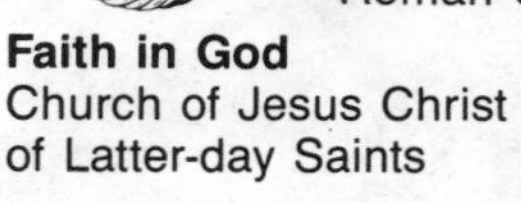

Parvuli Dei
Roman Catholic

Faith in God
Church of Jesus Christ of Latter-day Saints

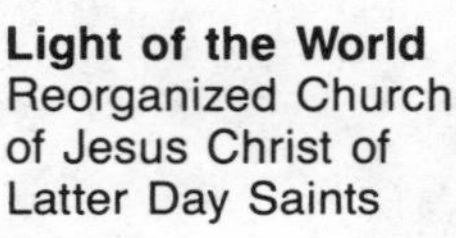

Light of the World
Reorganized Church of Jesus Christ of Latter Day Saints

Silver Crest
The Salvation Army

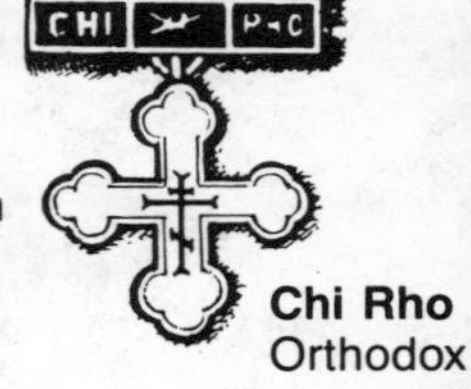

Chi Rho
Orthodox

WOLF TRAIL Akela's OK ____________ Date ____________ Recorded by den leader

ACHIEVEMENT

12 Using Books

Go to a public library with a grown-up. Find out how to get your own library card. Name four kinds of books that interest you.

I read ______________________________

____

____

____

WOLF TRAIL Akela's OK	Date	Recorded by den leader

Pick a book on a subject you like and read it. Tell a grown-up some things about it.

WOLF TRAIL Akela's OK	Date	Recorded by den leader

Books are important. Show that you know how to take care of them. Open a new book the right way. Make a paper or plastic cover for it or another book.

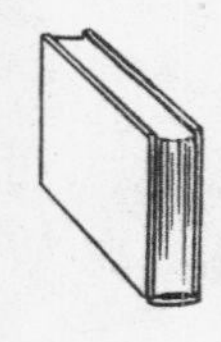

1
Hold the book on a table.

2
Let go of one cover and then the other.
Put the covers down gently. Keep the leaves closed and upright. Now take a few leaves at a time and lightly press them down.

3
Cut paper 3 inches bigger than the book.

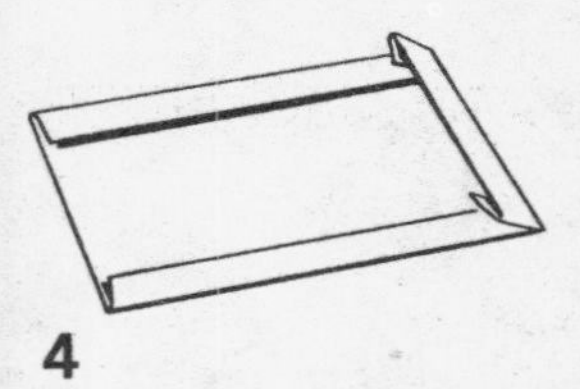

4
Fold top, bottom, and right side.

5
Slip the back cover into the right side fold. Make a fold for the front cover. Open the book and slip the front cover into the fold.

52

WOLF TRAIL Akela's OK ________ Date ________ Recorded by den leader

When you have filled in

48 of my tracks
through all 12 parts
of the WOLF trail,
you have earned the right
to wear my BADGE.

You are now a

WOLF CUB SCOUT!

ARROWHEAD TRAIL

NOW, you can earn

GOLD
arrow point

and

SILVER
arrow points.

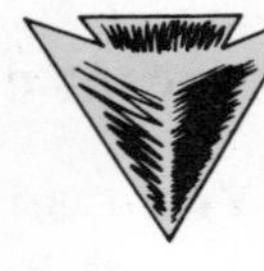

This arrowhead
tells you what to do.

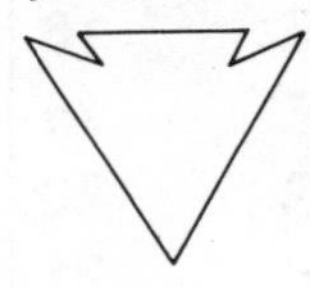

Fill in this arrowhead
when you have done it.

For any 10 filled-in arrowheads
you can get your

GOLD
Arrow Point

and 10 more your

SILVER
Arrow Point

and 10 more another

SILVER
Arrow Point

and so on . . . . .

ELECTIVE

Secret Codes

Learn to send messages so nobody who isn't in on the secret can read them. Learn to "talk" with your hands.

Use a secret code.

You can use numbers for letters.

1	A	14	N
2	B	15	O
3	C	16	P
4	D	17	Q
5	E	18	R
6	F	19	S
7	G	20	T
8	H	21	U
9	I	22	V
10	J	23	W
11	K	24	X
12	L	25	Y
13	M	26	Z

13 25 14 1 13 5 9 19 10 9 13
M Y N A M E I S J I M

23 8 1 20 9 19 25 15 21 18 19?

ARROWHEAD TRAIL Akela's OK Date ______ Recorded by den leader ______

Or turn alphabet upside down.

A	Z	N	M
B	Y	O	L
C	X	P	K
D	W	Q	J
E	V	R	I
F	U	S	H
G	T	T	G
H	S	U	F
I	R	V	E
J	Q	W	D
K	P	X	C
L	O	Y	B
M	N	Z	A

R ZN VRTSG
I AM EIGHT

SLD LOW ZIV BLF?

DSZG RH BLFI OZHG MZNV?

My code is________________________________

ARROWHEAD TRAIL Akela's OK Date — Recorded by den leader

Write to a friend in invisible "ink."

To make the ink, use 

or 
lemon juice.

Jim —
Meet me
after school
today —
Pete

Use a toothpick for a pen.

When the "ink" dries, you can't see it, until

You hold it over a light. The heat from the light will turn the "ink" light brown."

ARROWHEAD TRAIL Akela's OK Date ____________ Recorded by den leader ____________

"Write" your name with the alphabet of the deaf.

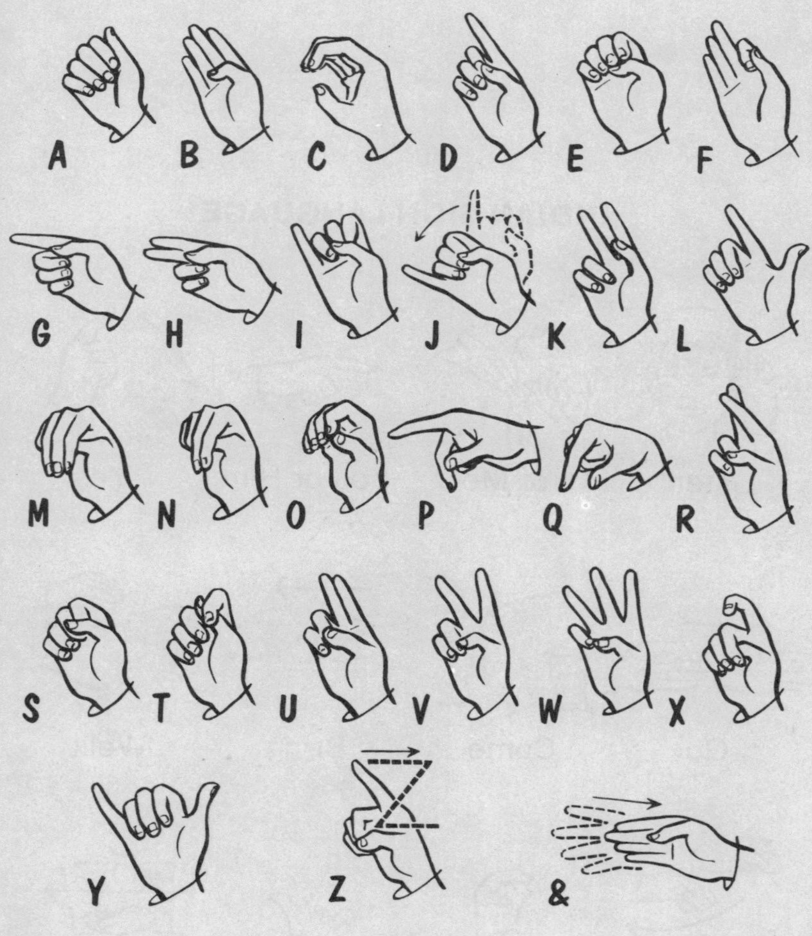

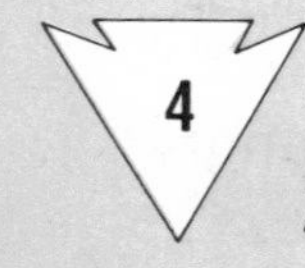

ARROWHEAD TRAIL Akela's OK Date

Recorded by den leader

Use 12 Indian signs to tell a story.

INDIAN SIGN LANGUAGE

Take
Run
With
Day
Eat
Drink
Sleep
Water
Friend
Talk
Man
Woman
Mind
Scout
Sunrise
Tongue
Heart
Good
Brave
True

What does this say?

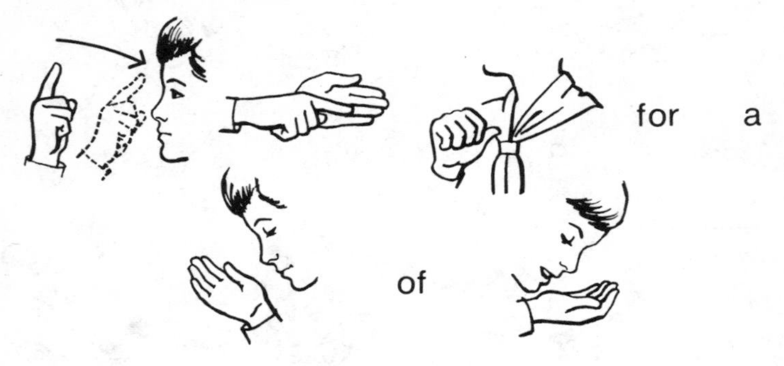

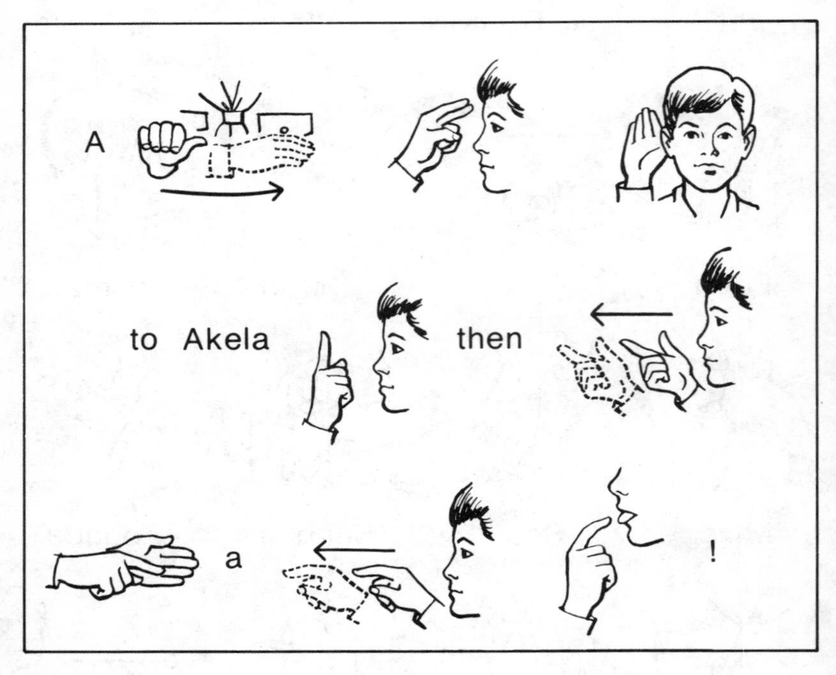

ARROWHEAD TRAIL Akela's OK Date Recorded by den leader

ELECTIVE

2 Dramatics

Be an actor, stage or costume designer. Find out what it is like to be on TV or in the movies.

Help to plan and put on a skit with costumes.

NOTE for Akela: Use ideas from TV and movies.

6

ARROWHEAD TRAIL Akela's OK Date ____ Recorded by den leader ____

Make some scenery for a den skit.

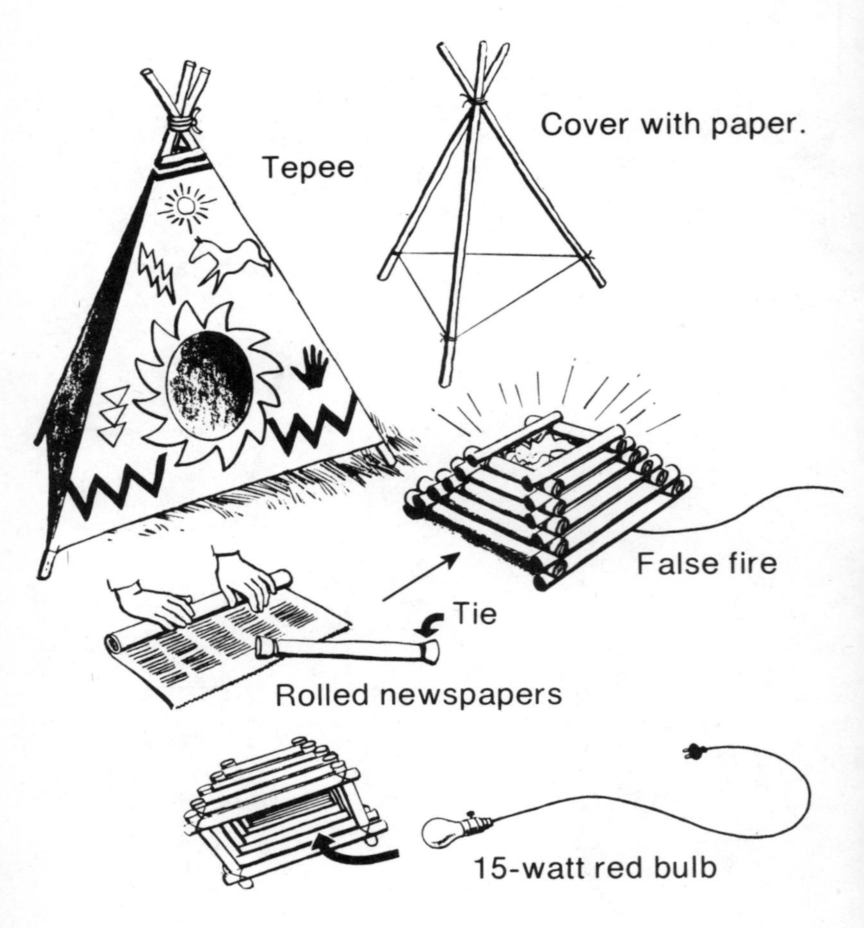

ARROWHEAD TRAIL Akela's OK Date

Recorded by den leader

Make sound effects for a den skit. Here are some ways to do it:

NOTE for Akela: Make these sounds behind a door or a screen so that the audience will think they are real.

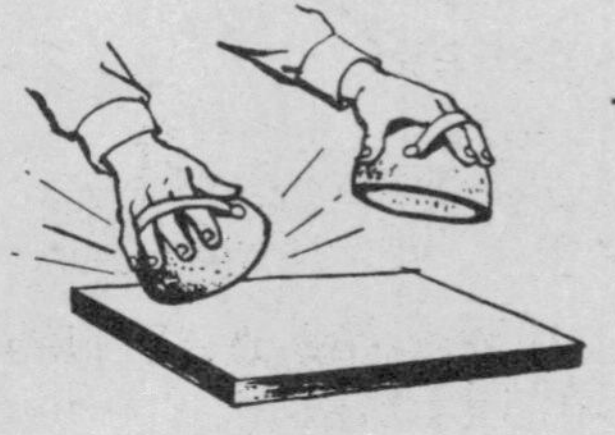

1 Pound plastic bowls on a board for the clop clop sound of horses.

2 Roll dried peas in a pan for rain.

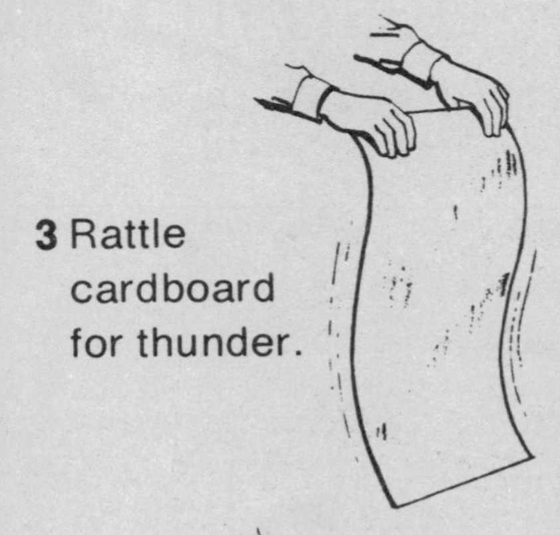

3 Rattle cardboard for thunder.

4 Slap floor or table for gunshot.

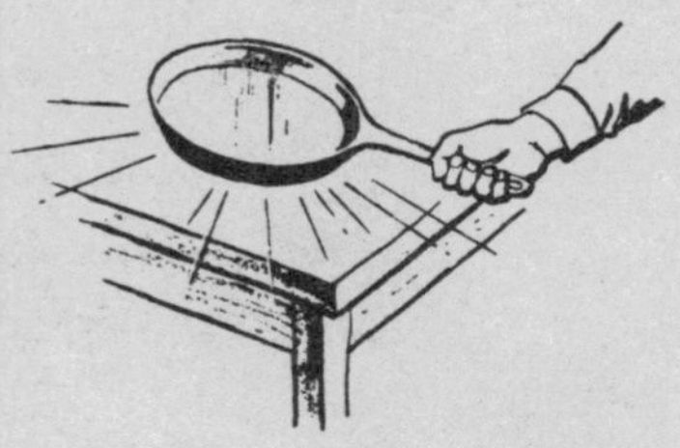

Use a bicycle bell for a telephone ring.

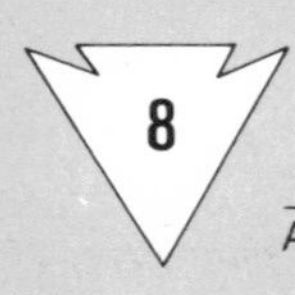

ARROWHEAD TRAIL Akela's OK Date _______________ Recorded by den leader _______________

Be the announcer for a den skit.

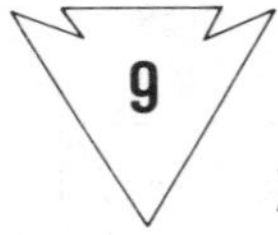

ARROWHEAD TRAIL Akela's OK Date

Recorded by den leader

Make a paper sack mask for a skit.

ARROWHEAD TRAIL Akela's OK Date

Recorded by den leader

ELECTIVE **3**

Handicraft

Watch carpenters and craftsmen at work. Learn how to handle tools; then pick a project and do it.

Make something useful for your home, church, or school.

Try one of the projects on pages 99–102.

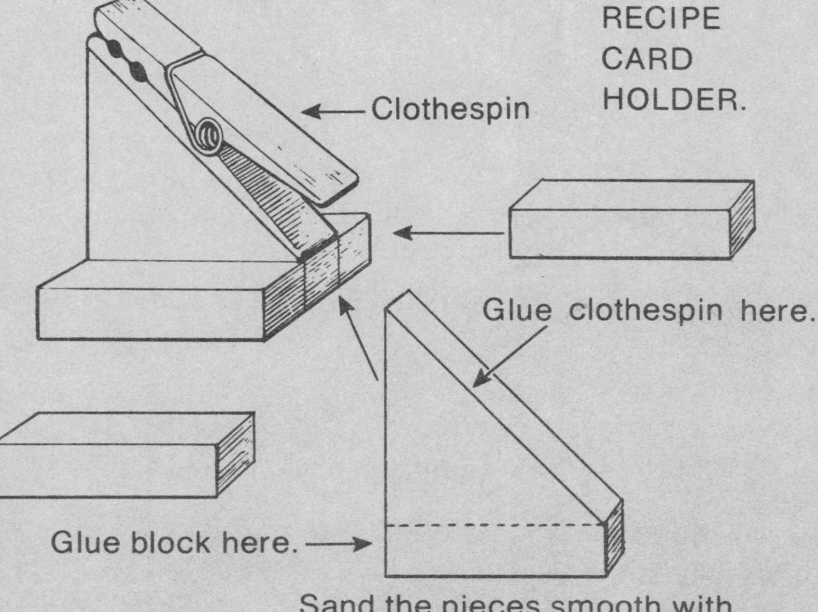

Sand the pieces smooth with sandpaper or steel wool before you put them together.

ARROWHEAD TRAIL Akela's OK Date ________ Recorded by den leader ________

A "CM" RULER.

How far can you
stretch your hand?

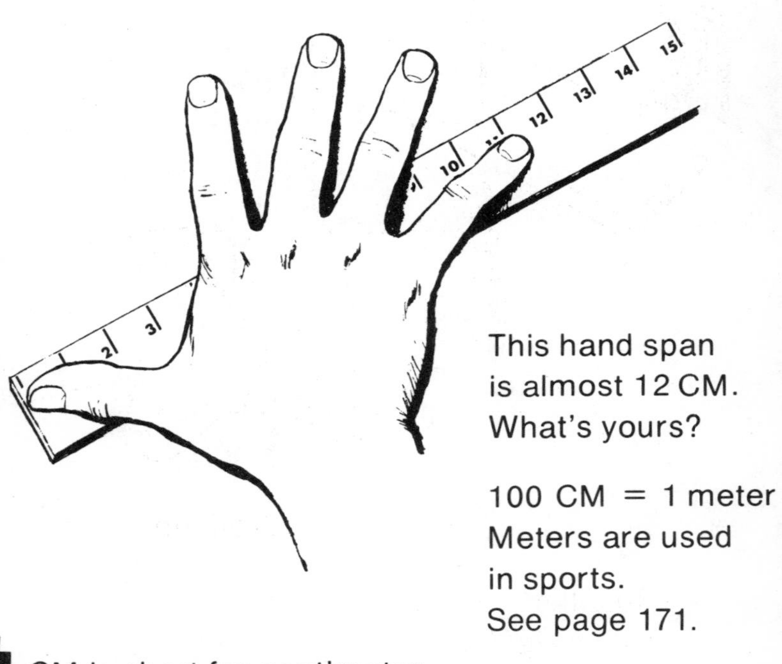

This hand span
is almost 12 CM.
What's yours?

100 CM = 1 meter
Meters are used
in sports.
See page 171.

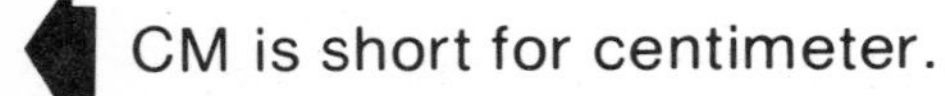

CM is short for centimeter.

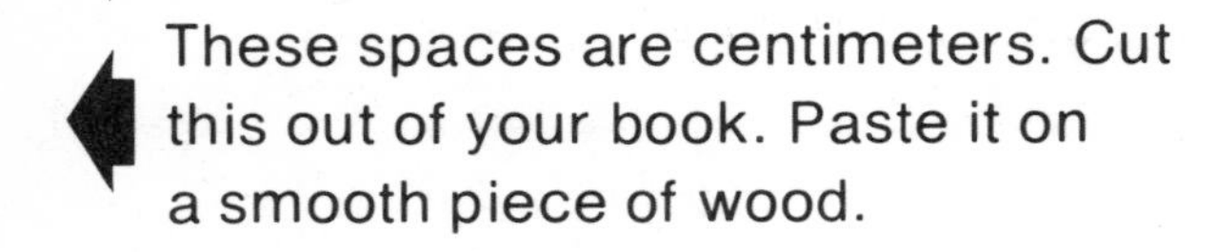

These spaces are centimeters. Cut
this out of your book. Paste it on
a smooth piece of wood.

ARROWHEAD TRAIL Akela's OK Date ______ Recorded by den leader ______

A BENCH FORK.

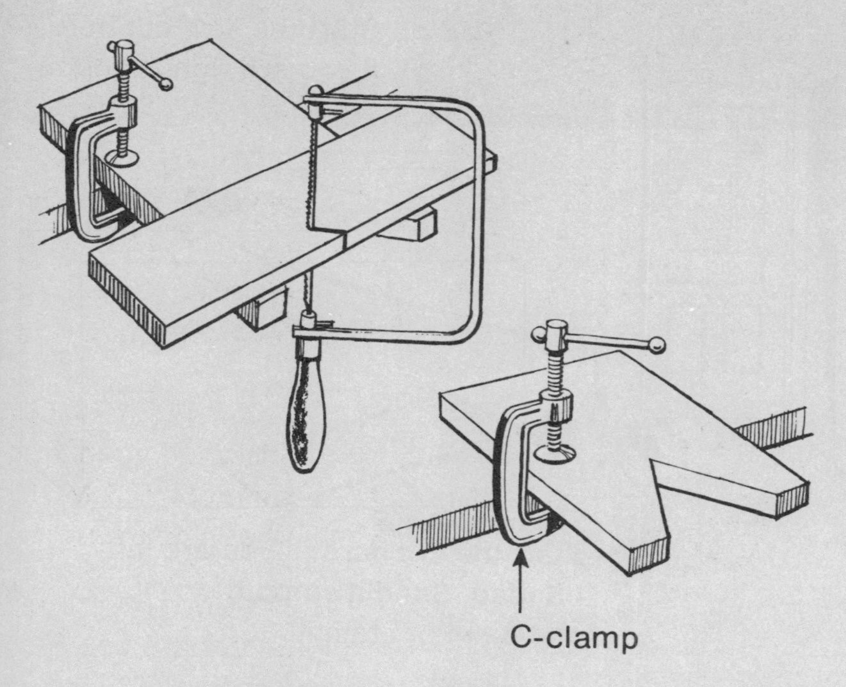

Hold the piece on the fork and cut straight up and down with a coping saw. The fork lets you move the piece around to cut curves.

ARROWHEAD TRAIL Akela's OK Date

Recorded by den leader

A DOOR STOP.

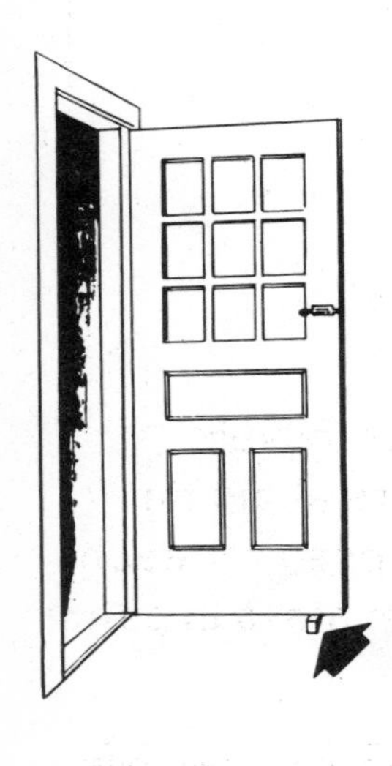

Start the saw cut here, if you are right-handed

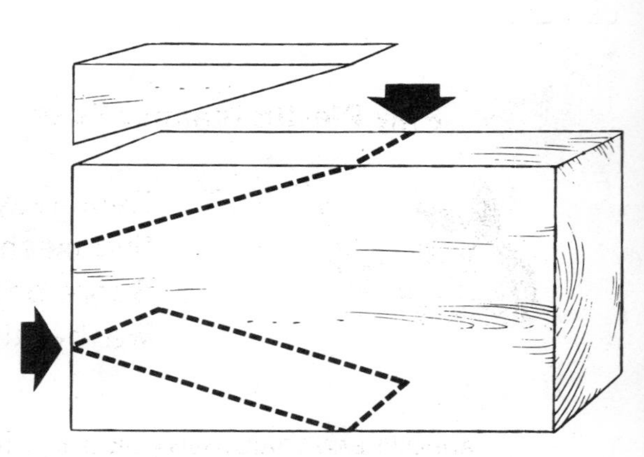

Start the cut here, if you are left-handed. Sand it smooth and paint or stain it.

ARROWHEAD TRAIL Akela's OK Date ______ Recorded by den leader ______

OR SOMETHING ELSE

I made a ____________________

ARROWHEAD TRAIL Akela's OK Date ______ Recorded by den leader ______

ELECTIVE

Games

Play these games with children younger than you are, with other Cub Scouts, or with grown-ups.

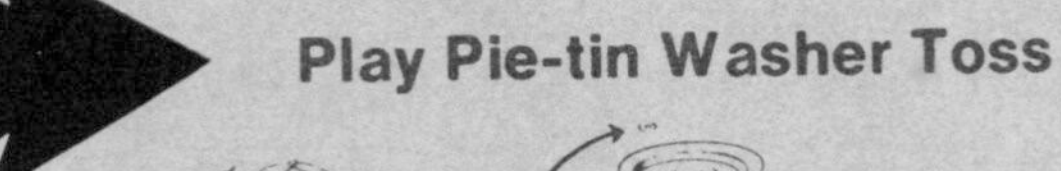

Play Pie-tin Washer Toss

Each player tosses five washers at pie tin. Score one point for each washer that stays in pan.

ARROWHEAD TRAIL Akela's OK Date ______ Recorded by den leader ______

Play Marble Sharpshooter

Each player rolls five marbles at soda-bottle targets. One point for each marble that rolls between bottles and misses them.

ARROWHEAD TRAIL Akela's OK Date ______ Recorded by den leader ______

Play the Hat Exchange Game

Make a circle
with players facing in.
Each player has a hat.

On the count of "one," take hold of the hat on the player on your right. On the count of "two," put it on your head.

When your leader says, "three," grab the hat on your left. At "four," put it on your head. Keep it up. Hats will move as numbers are changed.

ARROWHEAD TRAIL Akela's OK Date   Recorded by den leader

Play Ring Toss

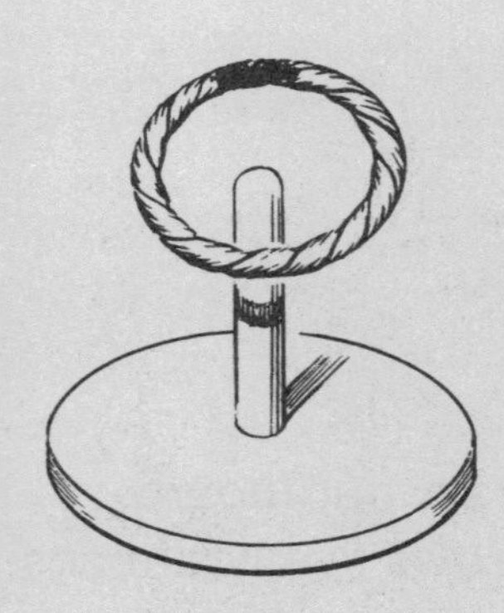

Make five rings out of rope, rubber, wire, heavy cardboard or folded newspaper.

Toss at stick in the ground or on a stand.

Ringers = 3 points
Leaners = 1 point

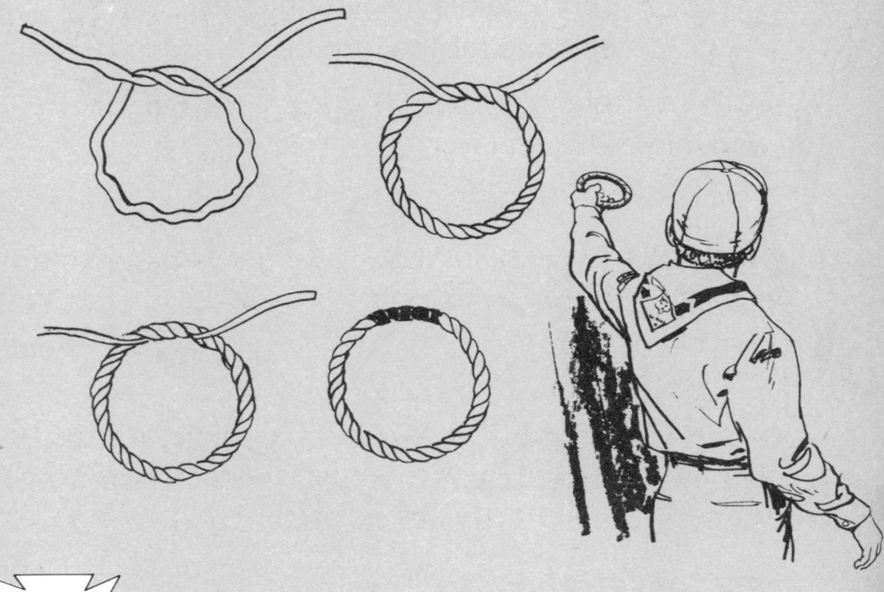

ARROWHEAD TRAIL Akela's OK Date ______ Recorded by den leader ______

Play a Beanbag Toss Game

Make a target out of heavy cardboard.
Color it. Each player throws five beanbags.
Three points for hitting eyes,
and one for the mouth.

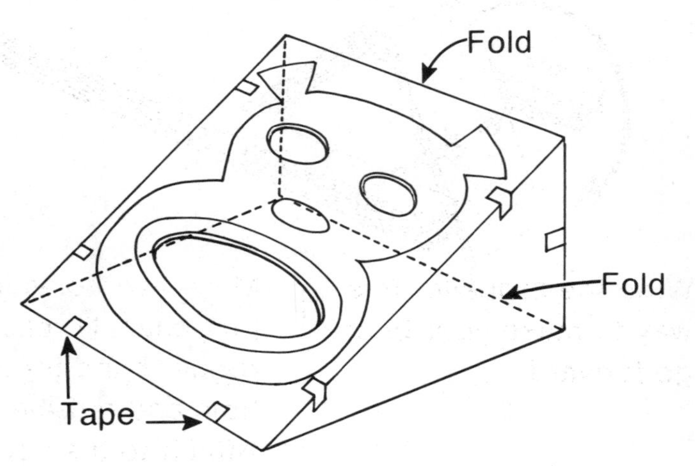

ARROWHEAD TRAIL Akela's OK Date ________ Recorded by den leader ________

ELECTIVE

Model Boats

Experts learn about boats by making small ones. Before a new kind of boat is built, a model is made to see how it behaves in the water.

Make a model boat with a rubber-band propeller.

Wind the propeller this way to make your boat go forward.

Make two holes in the propeller. Thread the rubber band through one hole and out the other. Attach to the boat. Wind it up, and let it go!

ARROWHEAD TRAIL Akela's OK Date   Recorded by den leader

Make or put together some kind of model boat.

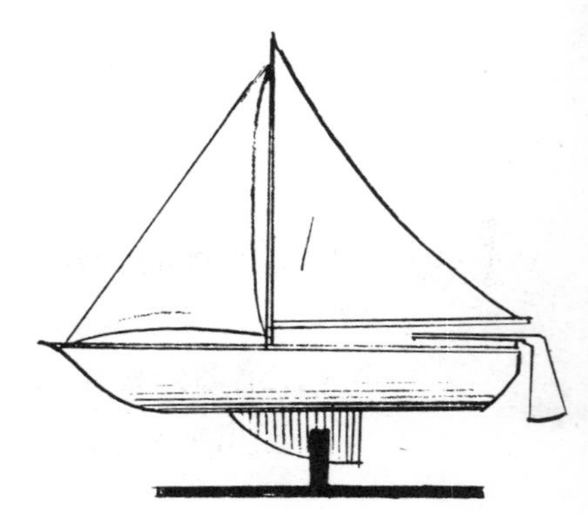

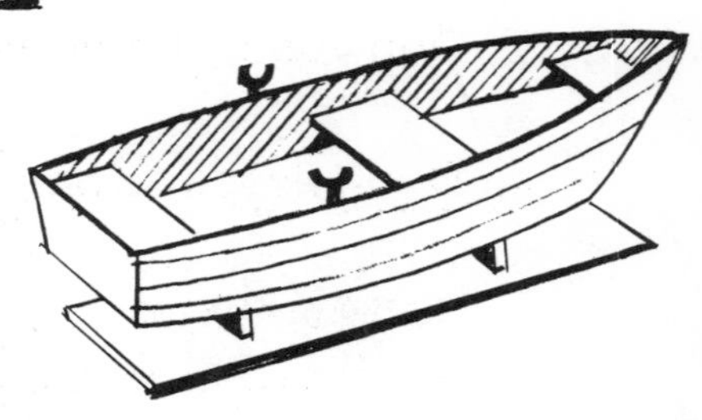

You can get credit each time you make a different model boat.

ARROWHEAD TRAIL Akela's OK Date

Recorded by den leader

ELECTIVE

Kites

Ride the wind with a kite you've made yourself. Do it safely. Watch how others fly kites, then try it yourself.

Explain safety rules for kite flying.

Never fly a kite near electric wires, buildings, ditches, or ponds.

Don't fly a kite in a thunderstorm.

Don't use metal in making a kite — it might attract lightning.

Don't use wire or wet string for a kiteline.

Don't fly a kite on a street or a railroad.

Don't try to get a kite that is caught in wires, treetops, roofs or high poles.

NOTE for Aleka: The danger of electric shock and of falling are lessened if these rules are followed.

ARROWHEAD TRAIL Akela's OK Date ______ Recorded by den leader ______

Make and fly a kite.

Make a paper-bag kite.

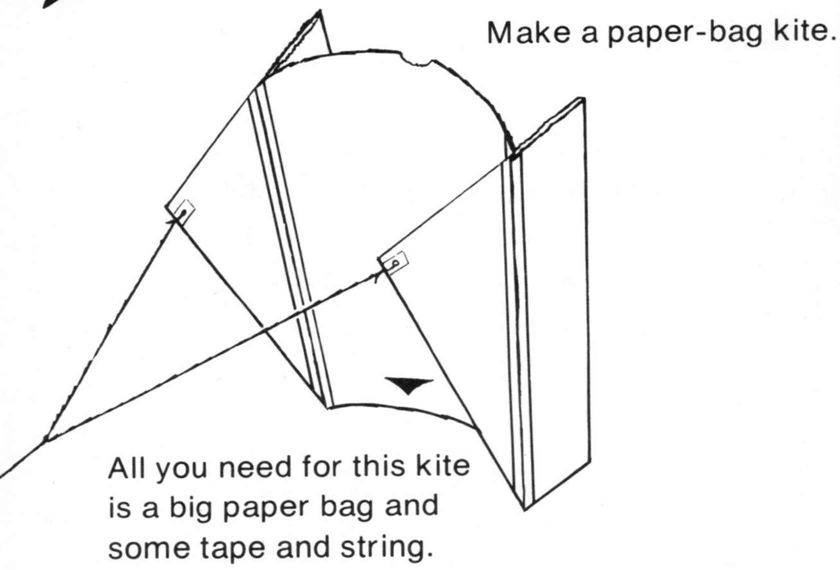

All you need for this kite is a big paper bag and some tape and string.

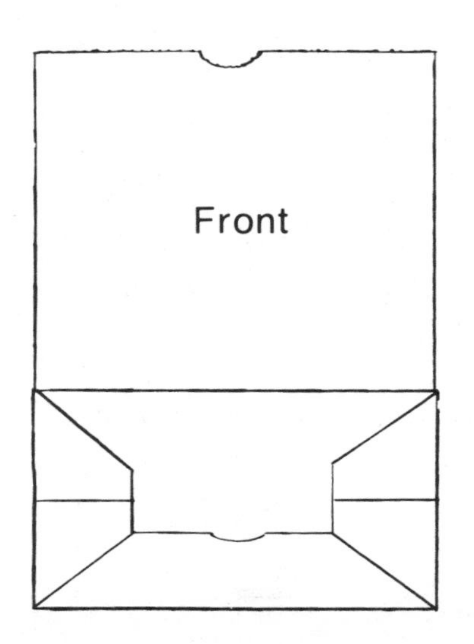

1 Cut out the bottom of the bag. Fold down the sides and make the bag flat.

2 Turn the bag over. Make a mark in the center of the bag a third of the way down. Draw lines to the corners and cut out the pieces on this side.

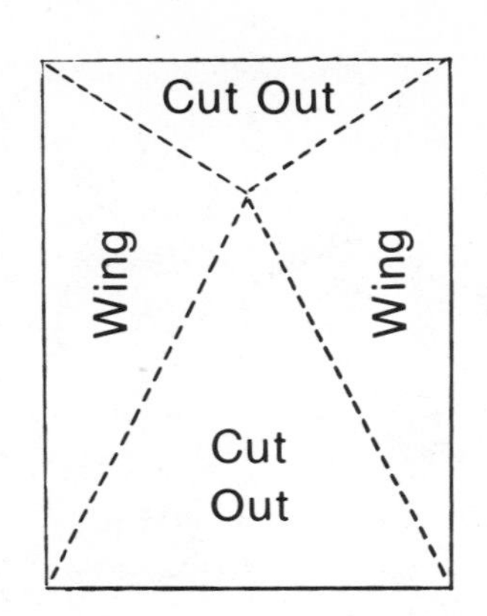

Folded side
Hole
Top Front
Hole
Tape
Wing
Tape
Wing
14cm
5cm
Vent

Some Cub Scouts tape a tail below the vent.

3 Turn the bag over and tape the wings and folded sides to the front. Tape the ends of the wings. Punch a hole in each wing through the tape for the strings. Cut out a vent near the bottom.

ARROWHEAD TRAIL Akela's OK Date ______ Recorded by den leader ______

OR Make a two-stick kite.

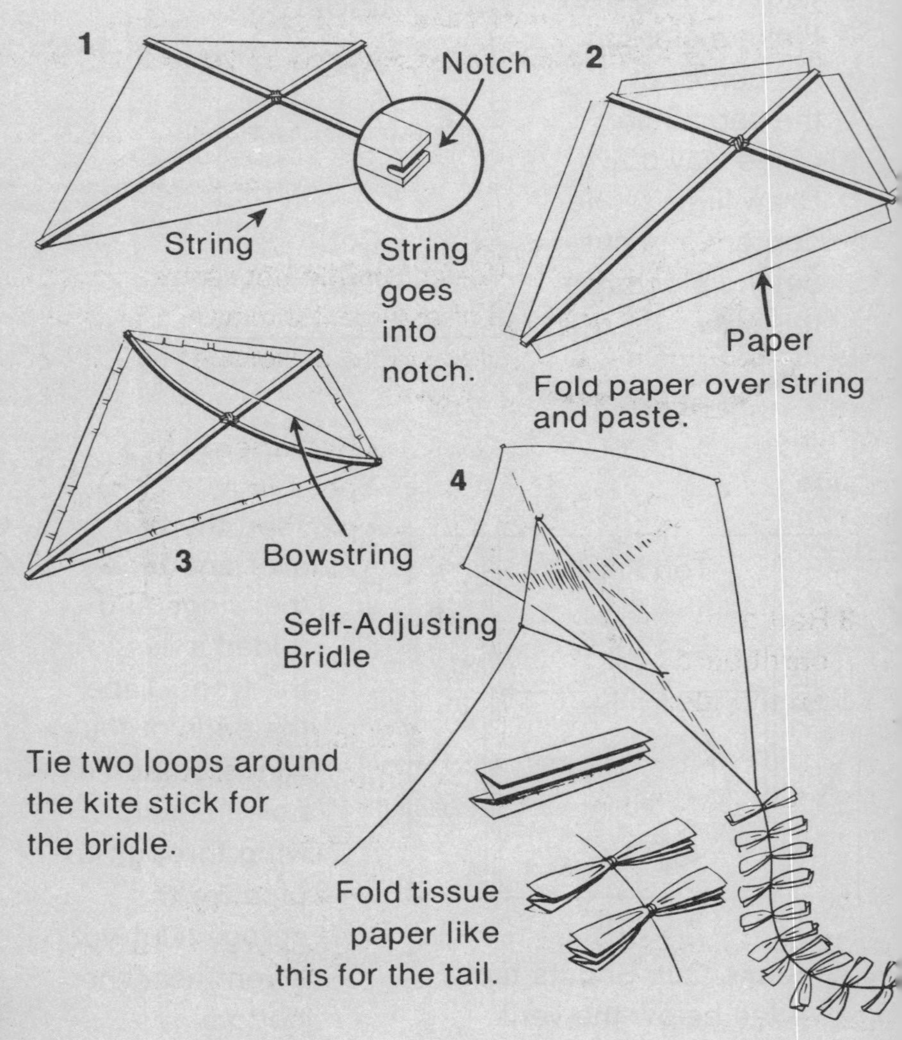

ARROWHEAD TRAIL Akela's OK Date ______ Recorded by den leader ______

OR Make a three-stick kite.

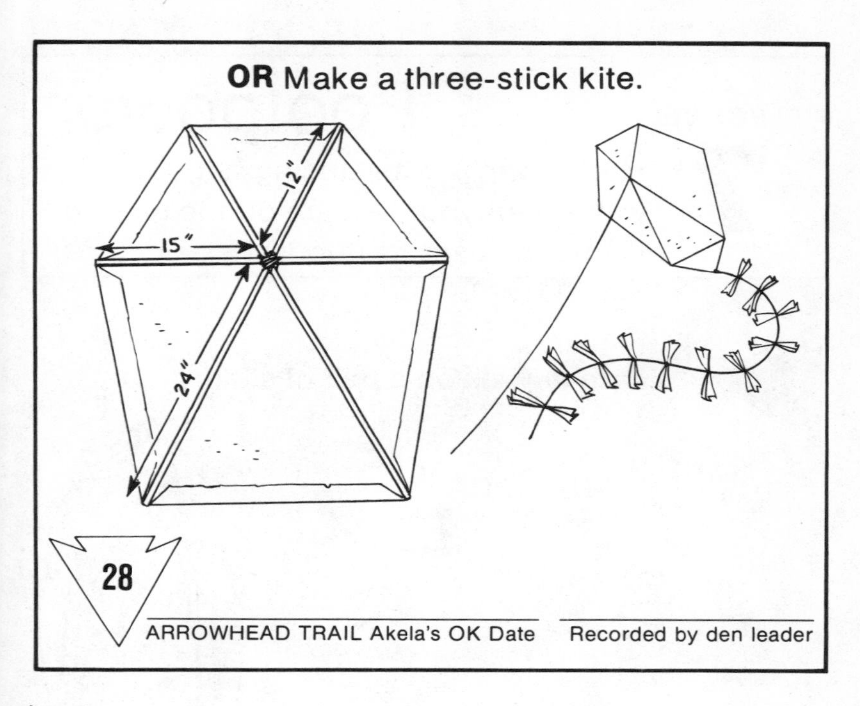

28

ARROWHEAD TRAIL Akela's OK Date   Recorded by den leader

Make and use a reel for kite string.

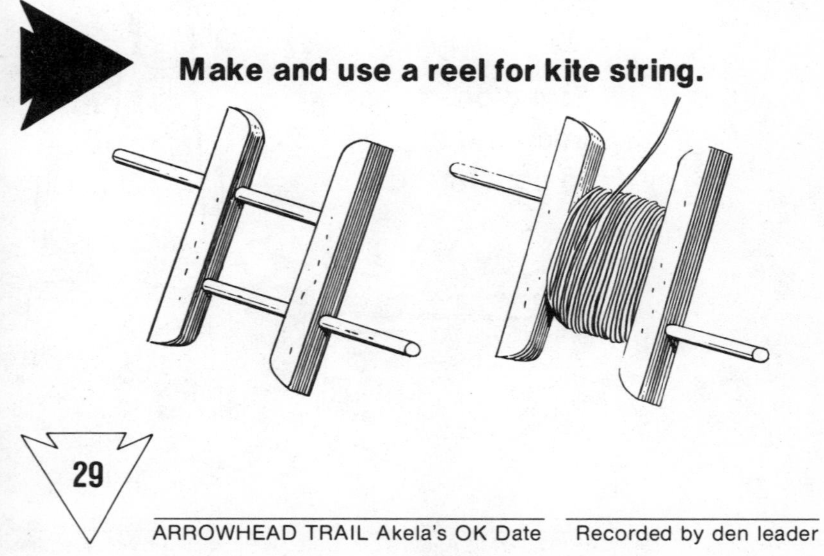

29

ARROWHEAD TRAIL Akela's OK Date   Recorded by den leader

ELECTIVE **7**

Footpower

Footpower is a balancing act. Can you walk when your feet are off the ground? It's not as hard as it looks!

Learn to walk on a pair of stilts.

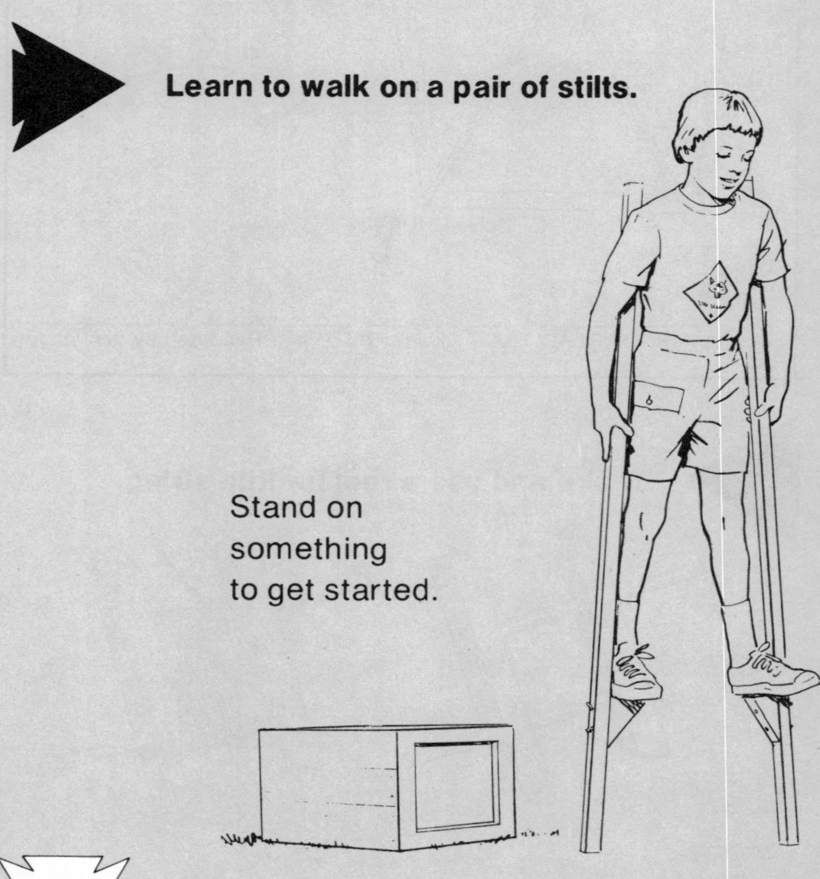

Stand on something to get started.

ARROWHEAD TRAIL Akela's OK Date

Recorded by den leader

Make a pair of "puddle jumpers" and walk with them.

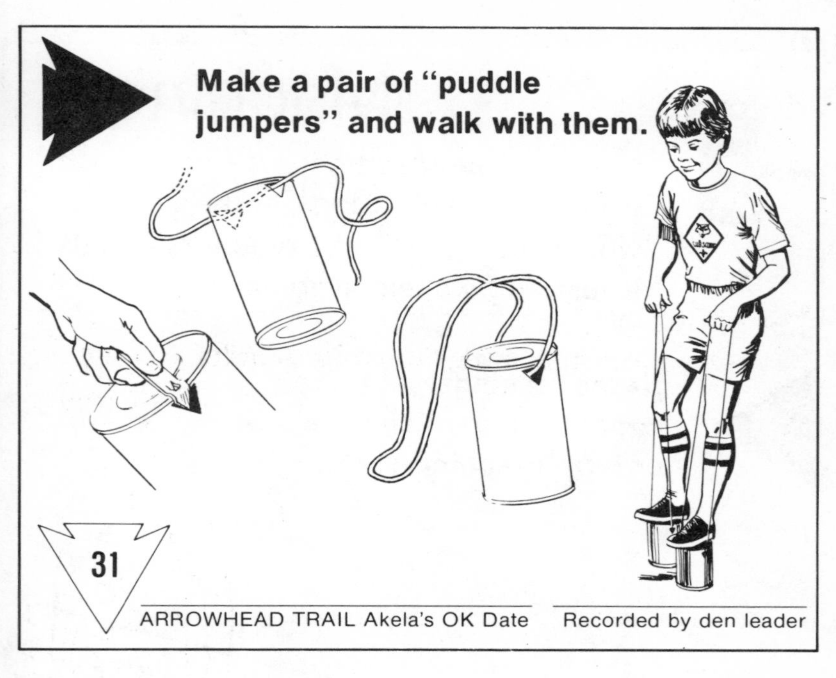

31

ARROWHEAD TRAIL Akela's OK Date   Recorded by den leader

Make a T-stick roller and race with it.

32

ARROWHEAD TRAIL Akela's OK Date   Recorded by den leader

ELECTIVE

8

Machinery

Learn about machines. A stick can be used as a lever, a log can be used as a wheel or a roller. Talk to workers who use levers and wheels everyday.

Name 10 kinds of trucks, construction machinery, or farm machinery.

NOTE to Akela: Encourage your Cub Scout to find pictures of machinery in newspapers and magazines. He can cut them out and paste them on these pages.

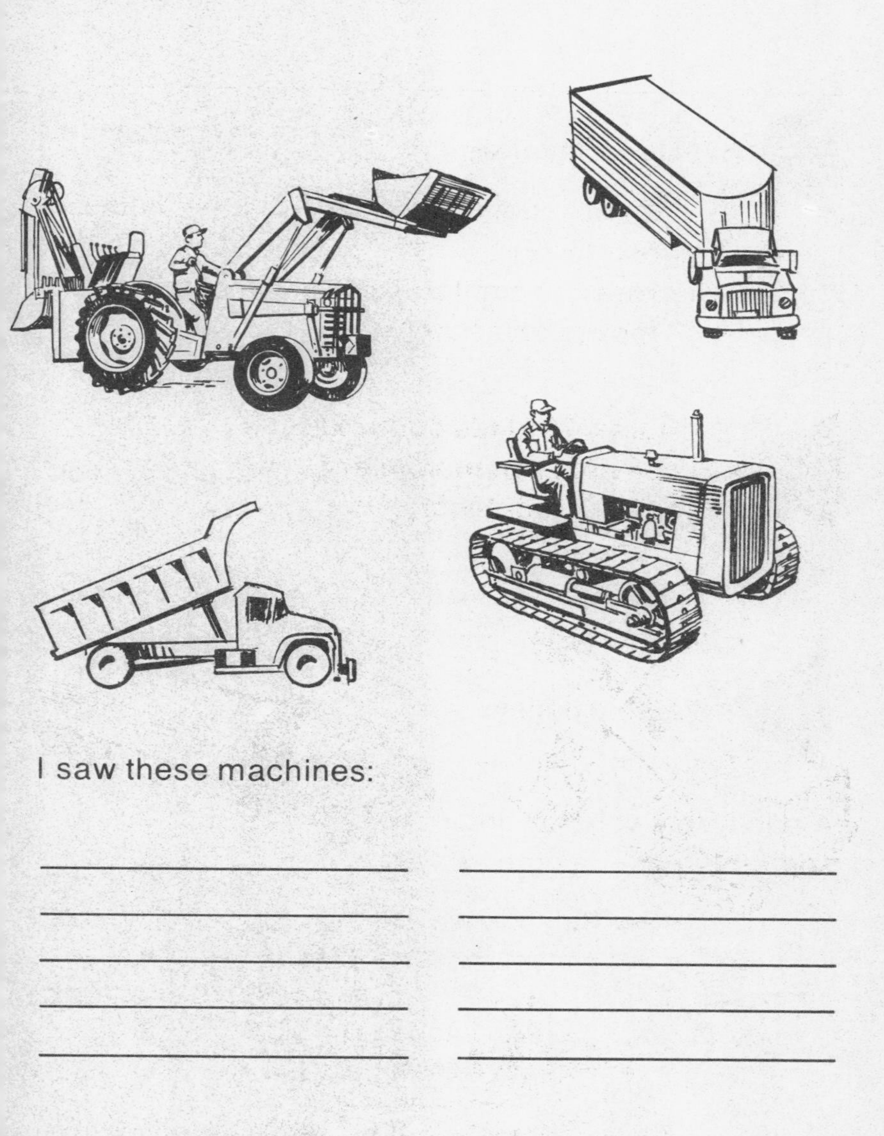

I saw these machines:

ARROWHEAD TRAIL Akela's OK Date

Recorded by den leader

Use a lever.

Push down here

Lever

Heavy weight moves up

Block of wood

When you pull out a nail,
the hammer handle is a lever.

ARROWHEAD TRAIL Akela's OK Date ________ Recorded by den leader ________

Use a pulley.

A pulley lets you pull and have
something go the other way.

Pull this way

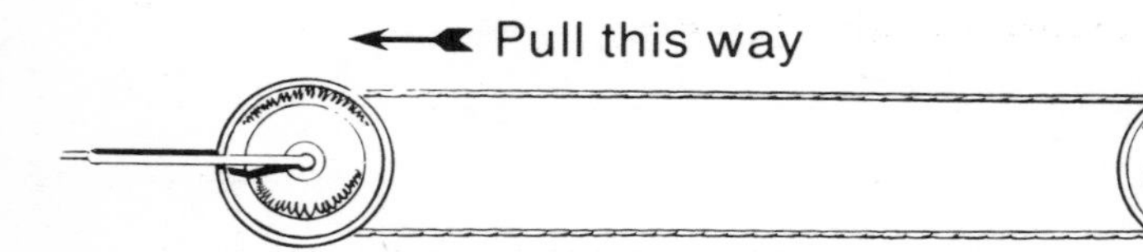

Line goes

Find some pulleys where you live.

ARROWHEAD TRAIL Akela's OK Date ________ Recorded by den leader ________

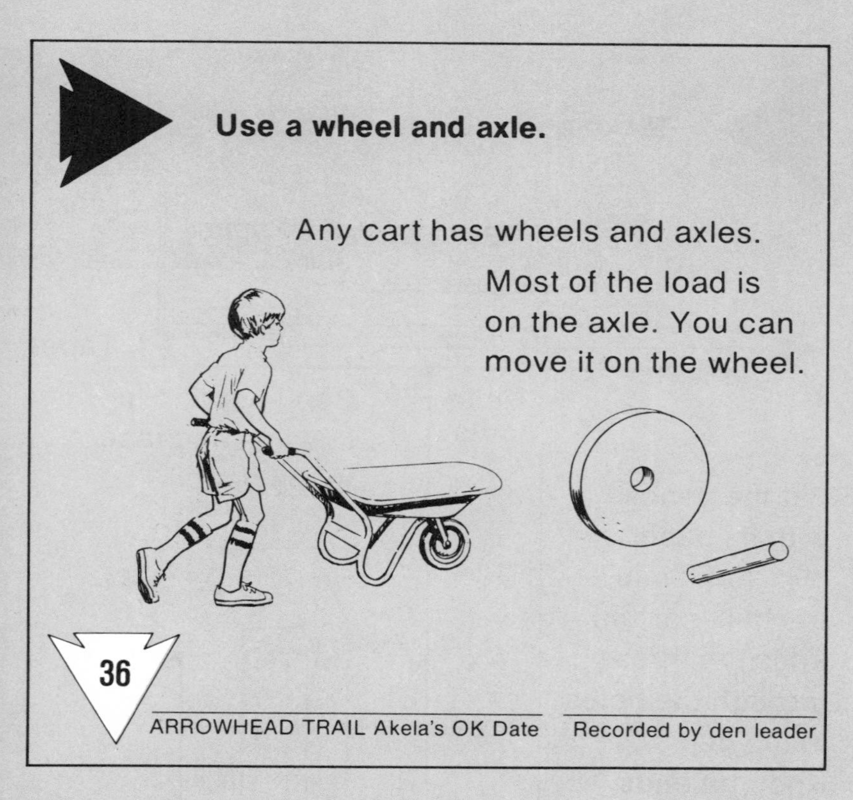

Use a wheel and axle.

Any cart has wheels and axles.

Most of the load is on the axle. You can move it on the wheel.

36

ARROWHEAD TRAIL Akela's OK Date ____________ Recorded by den leader ____________

Draw a plan for something and build it.

I made a ____

____

ARROWHEAD TRAIL Akela's OK Date ____________ Recorded by den leader ____________

Make and use a windlass.

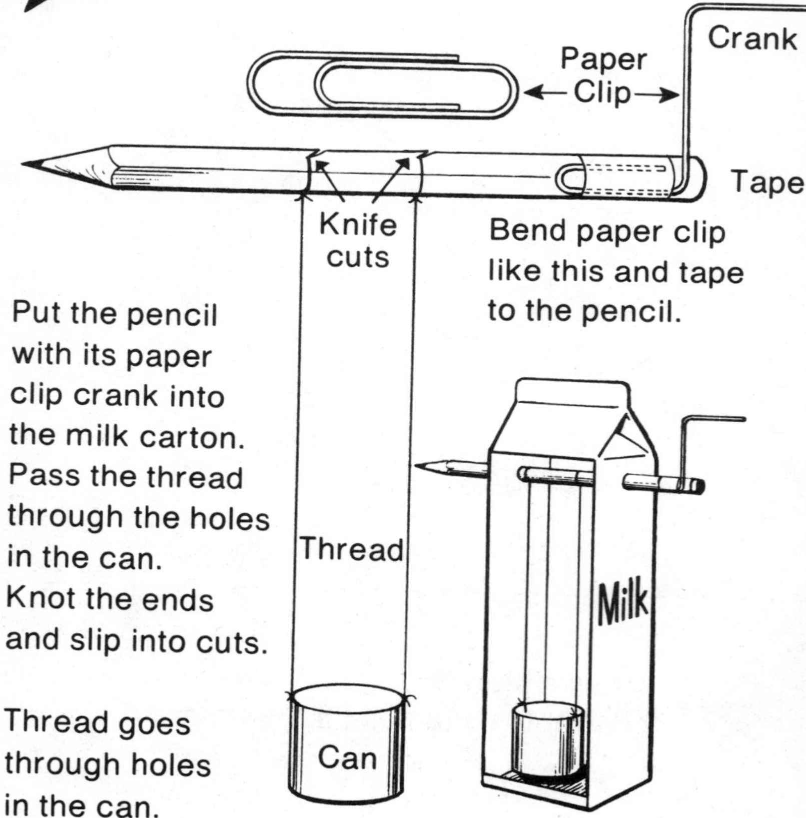

Bend paper clip like this and tape to the pencil.

Put the pencil with its paper clip crank into the milk carton. Pass the thread through the holes in the can. Knot the ends and slip into cuts.

Thread goes through holes in the can.

Cut one side from a milk carton. Punch holes for the pencil.

ARROWHEAD TRAIL Akela's OK Date ______ Recorded by den leader ______

ELECTIVE

Parties and Gifts

Parties are more fun when you've made a gift yourself and helped plan and put on the party.

Make a gift or toy like one of these and give it to someone.

Tin can pencil holder can be covered with string or paper and glued to the can.

Bean bag.

Use scrap cloth or an old pocket. Fill with dried beans. Fold in the top and sew shut.

I made a ____

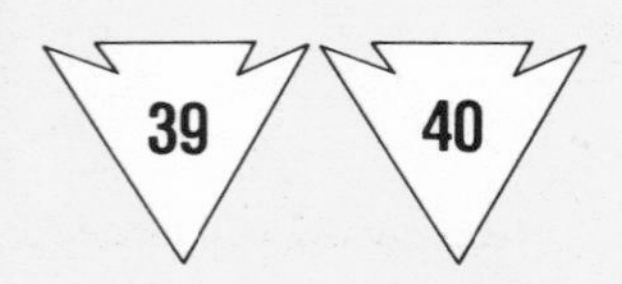

____
ARROWHEAD TRAIL Akela's OK Date

____
Recorded by den leader

Help with a home or den party.

Here are some of the things I did:

____

____

I helped decorate the room with

____

____

I helped plan and play these games

____

____

I helped serve refreshments.

We had______________________________

____

I helped clean up afterward by

____

____

ARROWHEAD TRAIL Akela's OK Date   Recorded by den leader

ELECTIVE **10**

Indians

The more you know about Indians, the more interested you will become.

Read a book about Indians.

I read ______________________________

ARROWHEAD TRAIL Akela's OK Date   Recorded by den leader

Learn and take part in an Indian dance.

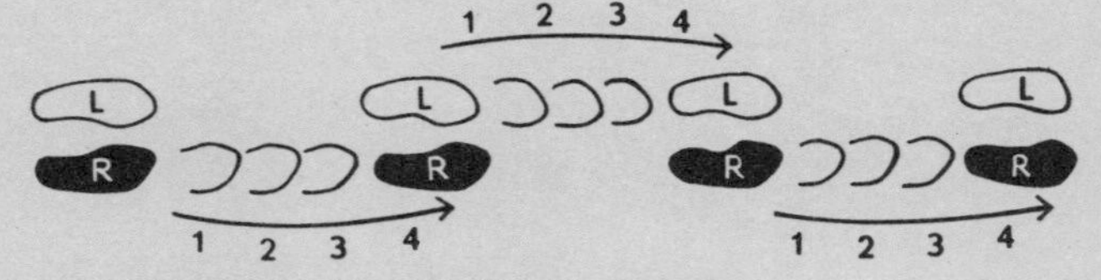

NOTE for Akela: The half steps mean that the Cub Scout just touches the ground with his foot. Count one, two, three, FOUR.

ARROWHEAD TRAIL Akela's OK Date   Recorded by den leader

Make an Indian tomahawk.

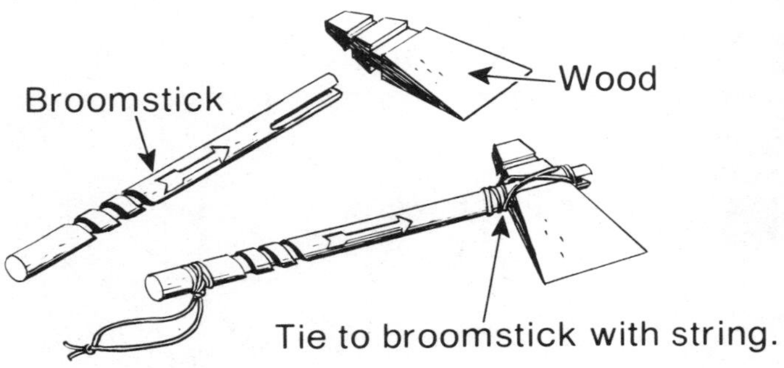

ARROWHEAD TRAIL Akela's OK Date ______ Recorded by den leader ______

Make an Indian spear.

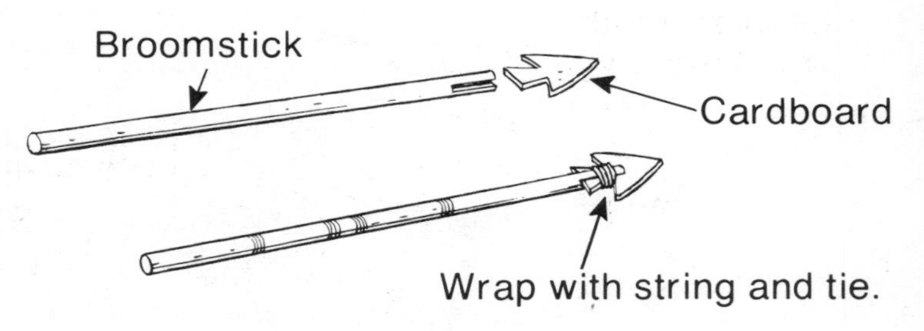

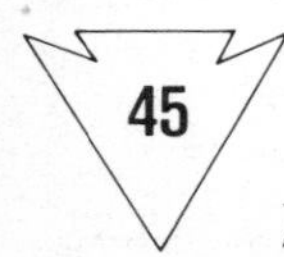

ARROWHEAD TRAIL Akela's OK Date ______ Recorded by den leader ______

Make an Indian bow and arrow.

NOTE for Akela: Cut green sticks from bushes.

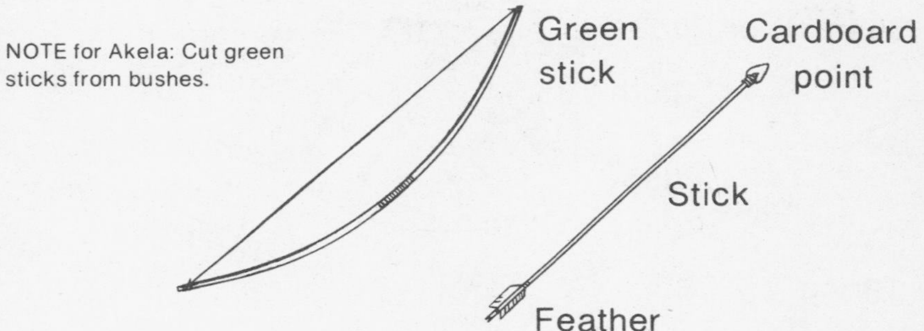

ARROWHEAD TRAIL Akela's OK Date ________ Recorded by den leader ________

Make a set of bell bands to wear on your legs or arms.

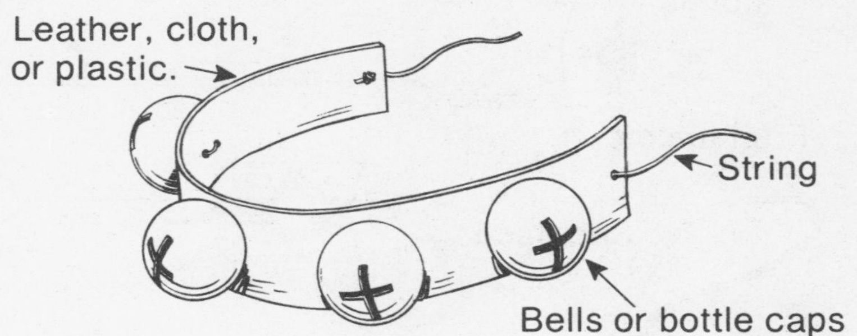

ARROWHEAD TRAIL Akela's OK Date ________ Recorded by den leader ________

Make an Indian tom-tom.

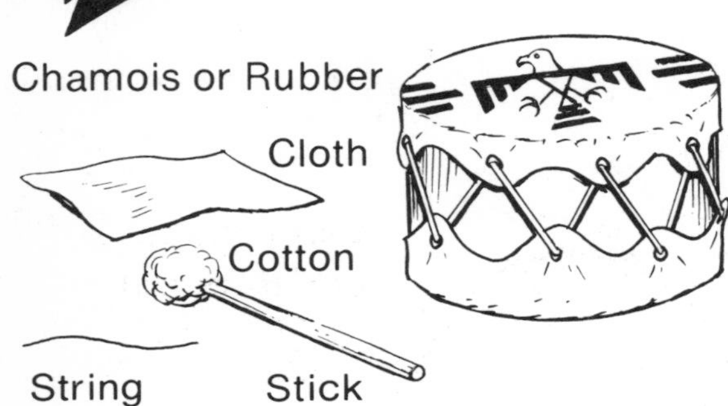

A big can
or something
round and hollow.

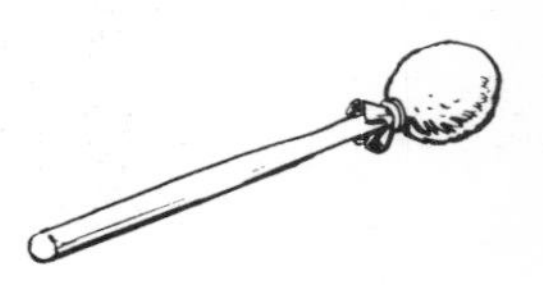

ARROWHEAD TRAIL Akela's OK Date ______ Recorded by den leader ______

Make an Indian rattle.

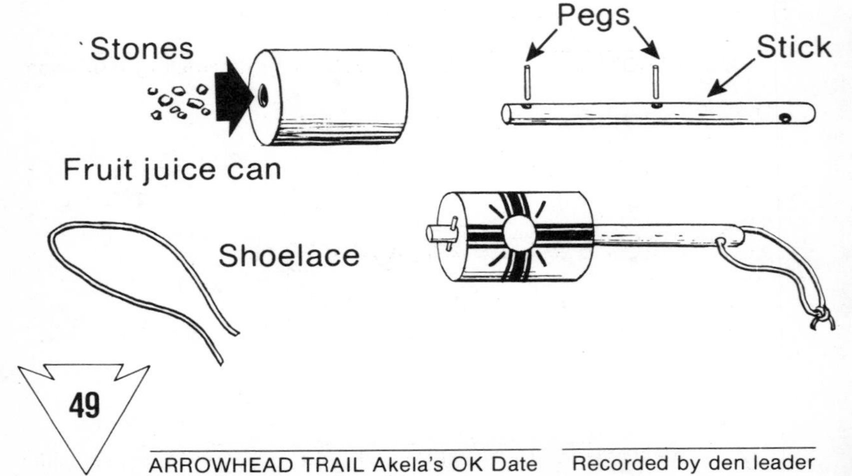

ARROWHEAD TRAIL Akela's OK Date ______ Recorded by den leader ______

Make an Indian shield.

ARROWHEAD TRAIL Akela's OK Date ______ Recorded by den leader ______

Make an Indian costume.

ARROWHEAD TRAIL Akela's OK Date ______ Recorded by den leader ______

Learn 12 word pictures and write a story with them.

Big voice

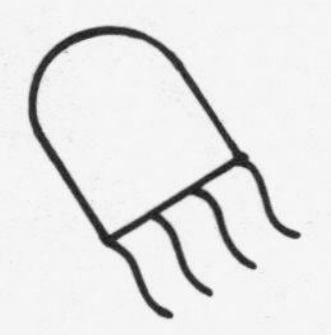

Bear alive

Bear dead

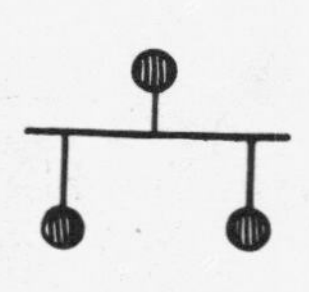

Bad

Top man

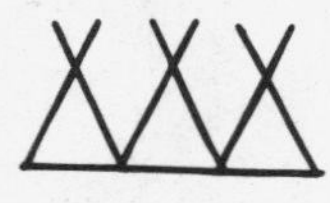

Camp

Brothers

Make peace

Council

Talk

Wise man

Hunt

Morning

Noon

Evening

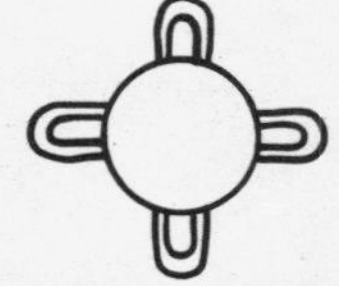

Directions

Man

Woman

Boy

Man on horse

ARROWHEAD TRAIL Akela's OK Date ______ Recorded by den leader ______

ELECTIVE

Songs

Learn to sing lots of songs. There are glad songs and sad songs; and some are proud like "The Star-Spangled Banner."

Learn and sing the first and last verses of "America."

My country, 'tis of thee,
Sweet land of liberty,
Of thee I sing;
Land where my fathers died,
Land of the Pilgrim's pride,
From every mountainside
Let freedom ring.

Our father's God, to Thee,
Author of liberty,
To thee we sing;
Long may our land be bright
With freedom's holy light,
Protect us by Thy might
Great God, our King.

ARROWHEAD TRAIL Akela's OK Date ________ Recorded by den leader ________

Learn and sing the first verse of the "Star-Spangled Banner"

O say, can you see
by the dawn's early light
What so proudly we hailed,
at the twilight's last gleaming,
Whose broad stripes and bright stars,
through the perilous fight,
O'er the the ramparts we watched,
were so gallantly streaming?
And the rockets' red glare
the bombs bursting in air,
Gave proof through the night
that our flag was still there!
O say, does that star-spangled
banner yet wave
O'er the land of the free
and the home of the brave?

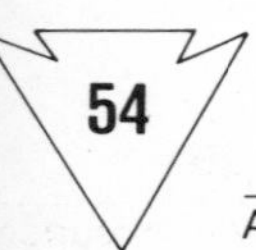

ARROWHEAD TRAIL Akela's OK Date ____ Recorded by den leader ____

Learn the words and sing three Cub Scout songs.

You can find other songs in the *Cub Scout Songbook.*

GOOD NIGHT, CUB SCOUTS.

Tune: "Good Night,Ladies"

Good night, Cub Scouts.
Good night, Cub Scouts.
Good night, Cub Scouts,
We're going to leave you now.

Merrily, we Cub along, Cub Along, Cub Along.
Merrily, we Cub along up the Cub Scout trail.

Sweet dreams, Cub Scouts.
Sweet dreams, Cub Scouts.
Sweet dreams, Cub Scouts,
We're going to leave you now.

I HAVE A DOG

Tune: "Reuben, Reuben, I've Been Thinking"

I have a dog, his name is Fido,
I have raised him from a pup.
He can stand upon his hind legs
If you hold his front legs up!

TRAIN SONG

Tune: "Yankee Doodle"

I met an engine on a hill
  All hot and broken-hearted,
And this is what he said to me
  As up the hill he started.

(Slowly)

I think I can, I think I can,
  At any rate, I'll try.
I think I can, I think I can,
  At any rate, I'll try.

He reached the top, and looking back
  To where he stood and doubted,
He started on the downward track
  And this is what he shouted:

(Faster)

I knew I could, I knew I could,
I never should have doubted.
I knew I could, I knew I could,
I never should have doubted!

I learned ____

____

____

ARROWHEAD TRAIL Akela's OK Date ____________ Recorded by den leader ____________

Learn the words and sing the first verse of three other songs, hymns, or prayers. Write the verse of one of the songs learned.

I learned

ARROWHEAD TRAIL Akela's OK Date

Recorded by den leader

ELECTIVE

Drawing

You can't tell if you can draw a picture until you try. Someday, you may become an artist or a draftsman.

Make a freehand sketch.

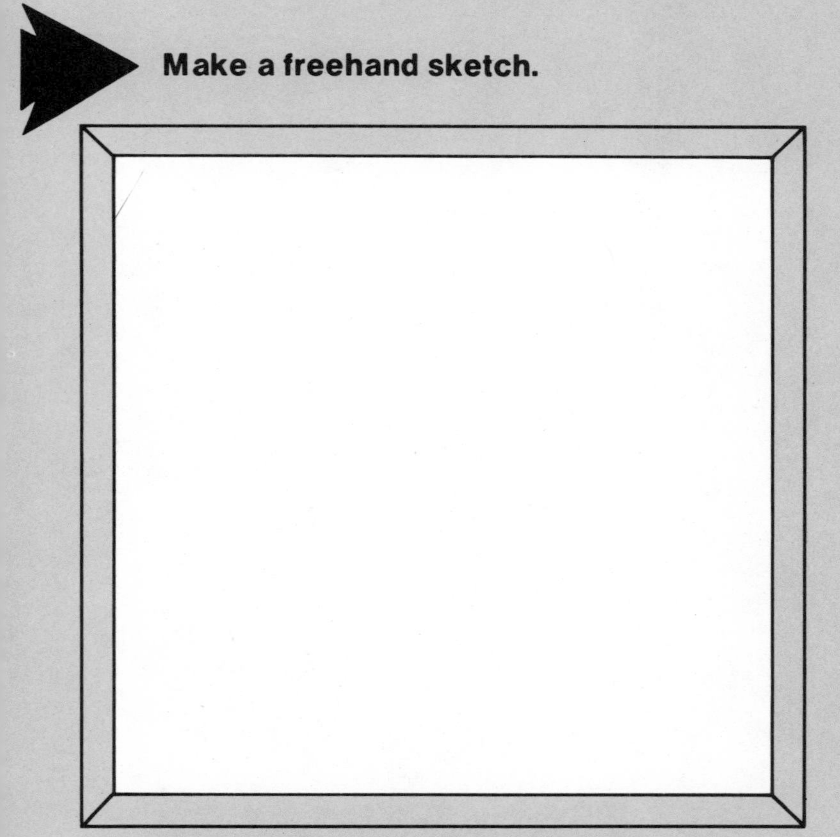

Draw anything you like here.

57

ARROWHEAD TRAIL Akela's OK Date   Recorded by den leader

Tell a story in three steps by drawing three cartoons.

ARROWHEAD TRAIL Akela's OK Date Recorded by den leader

Help draw, paint, or crayon some scenery for a den or pack skit or puppet show.

Use a large sheet of paper or cardboard.

City

Country

ARROWHEAD TRAIL Akela's OK Date ______ Recorded by den leader ______

Make a stencil pattern.

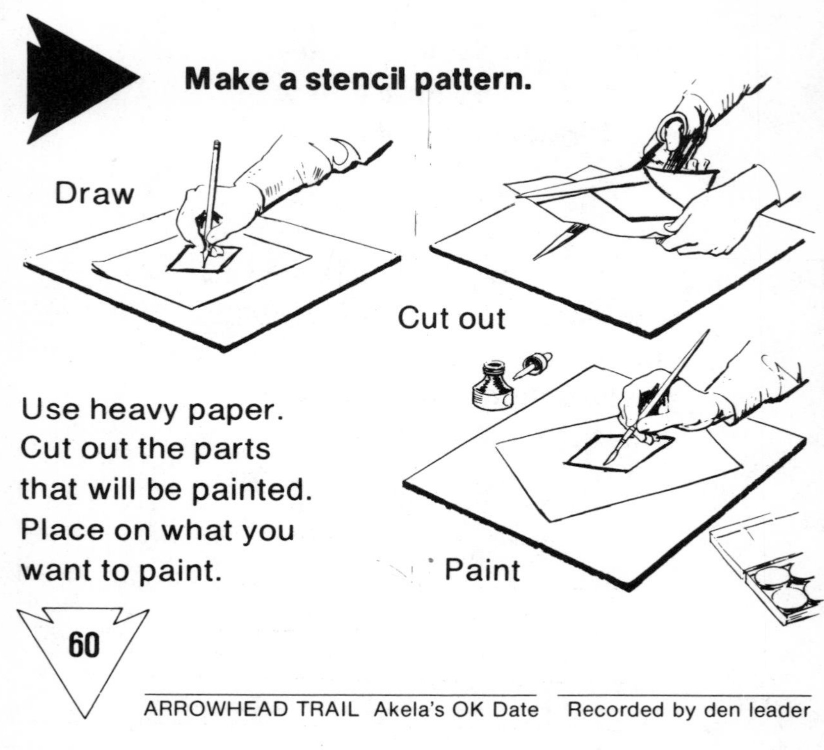

Use heavy paper.
Cut out the parts
that will be painted.
Place on what you
want to paint.

ARROWHEAD TRAIL Akela's OK Date ____________ Recorded by den leader ____________

Make a poster for a Cub Scout project or pack meeting.

ARROWHEAD TRAIL. Akela's OK Date ____________ Recorded by den leader ____________

ELECTIVE

13

Birds

Some birds follow the sun each year. These summer visitors need homes. The ones that stay behind need to be fed.

Make a list of all the birds you saw in a week and tell where you saw them (field, forest, marsh, yard, or park).

ARROWHEAD TRAIL Akela's OK Date

Recorded by den leader

Put out nesting material (yarn and string) for birds and tell what birds might use it.

ARROWHEAD TRAIL Akela's OK Date ____________ Recorded by den leader ____________

Read a book about birds.

I read ____

ARROWHEAD TRAIL Akela's OK Date ____________ Recorded by den leader ____________

Point out 10 different kinds of birds (5 may be from pictures).

ARROWHEAD TRAIL Akela's OK Date ____________ Recorded by den leader ____________

Feed wild birds and tell which birds you fed.

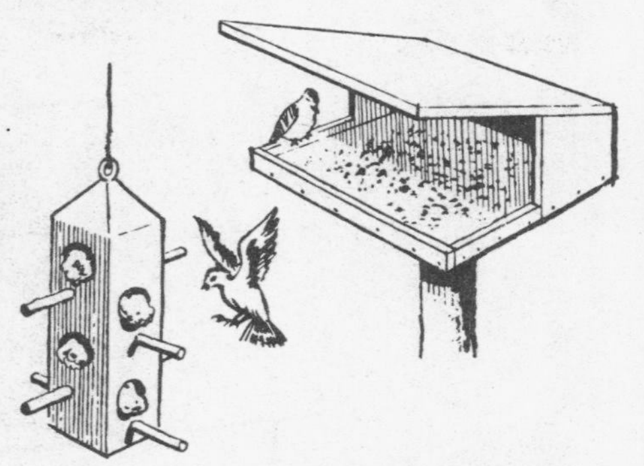

Feed birds all winter.

Birds like bread crumbs, cracked corn, sunflower seeds, millet, or other grains.
Make your own birdbath.
Keep birdbath clean.

ARROWHEAD TRAIL Akela's OK Date ____________ Recorded by den leader ____________

Put out a bird house and tell what birds use it.

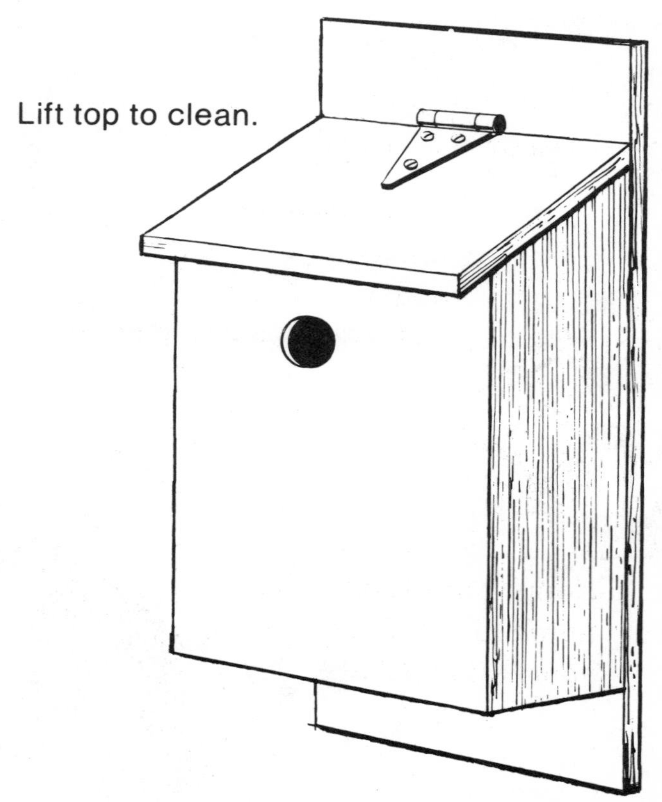

Clean out each year in the fall.

ARROWHEAD TRAIL Akela's OK Date ____ Recorded by den leader ____

ELECTIVE

14

Pets

Your pet may be a dog, cat, rabbit, parakeet, or a tropical fish. All pets need care—even crickets.

Take care of a pet.

Dogs need a clean place to live. Feed your dog dog food and water. Don't feed your dog small bones.

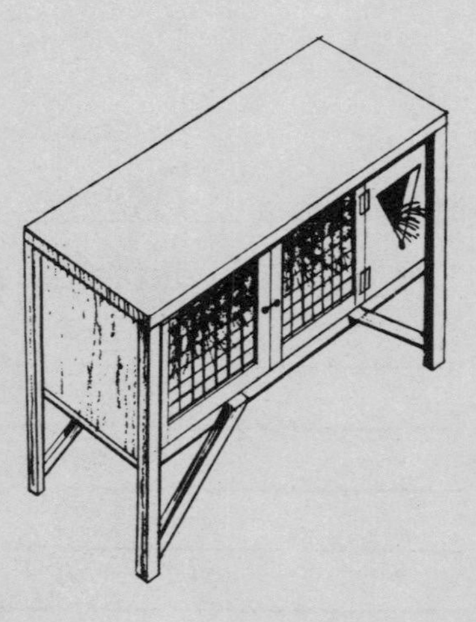

Keep your rabbit hutch clean. Feed your rabbit pellets.

Feed your bird birdseed, grit, and water.

Keep the cage clean.

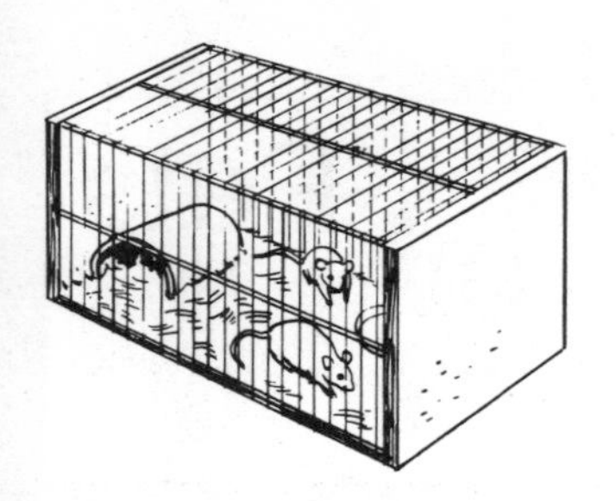

Gerbils, hamsters, guinea pigs, white mice, and rats need prepared food, nuts, seeds, and water. Clean the cage every day.

Feed fish prepared fish food, lettuce, cabbage, or celery leaves.

My pet is a ______________________________

This is what I did to take care of it:

____

____

____

____

____

ARROWHEAD TRAIL Akela's OK Date ______ Recorded by den leader ______

Tell what is meant by rabid. Tell what you should do if you see a dog or wild animal that acts as if it may be rabid.

Rabid means **sick!**

Don't go near wild animals that seem to be **TAME**.

Don't go near a dog that seems to be—

CHOKING

EXCITED

AFRAID

Tell a grown-up right away if you are bitten or scratched by any pet or wild animal.

ARROWHEAD TRAIL. Akela's OK Date ______ Recorded by den leader ______

Know what to do when you meet a strange dog.

If a dog comes up to you:

1. Stand still with your hands down. Let the dog sniff them.
2. Don't make any quick moves and don't pet him.
3. Don't try to scare him away or show that you are afraid.
4. Walk quietly away. **Don't** run.

ARROWHEAD TRAIL, Akela's OK Date ______ Recorded by den leader ______

Read a book about a pet and tell about it at a den meeting.

I read ______________________________

ARROWHEAD TRAIL Akela's OK Date ______ Recorded by den leader ______

ELECTIVE

15

Gardening

Growing a garden is almost like magic. You put tiny seeds in the ground, and presto, little green plants spring up.

Plant and raise a box garden.

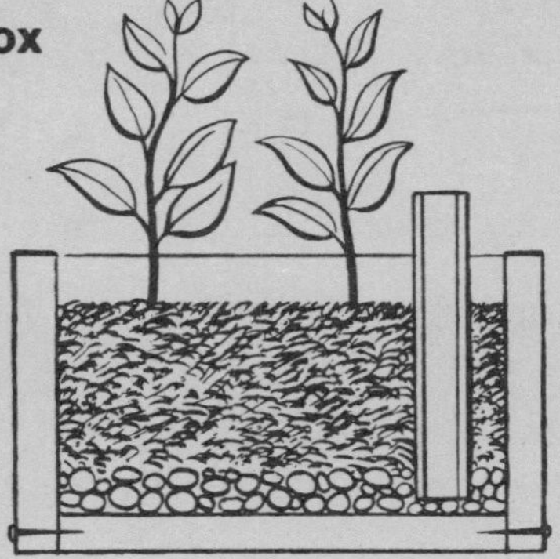

Put stones in the bottom and soil on the top. Pour water into the pipe.

ARROWHEAD TRAIL, Akela's OK Date ____________ Recorded by den leader ____________

Plant and raise a flower bed.

I grew ____

ARROWHEAD TRAIL Akela's OK Date ____________ Recorded by den leader ____________

Grow a plant indoors.

Pineapple Grapefruit Mimosa Avocado Sweet Potato

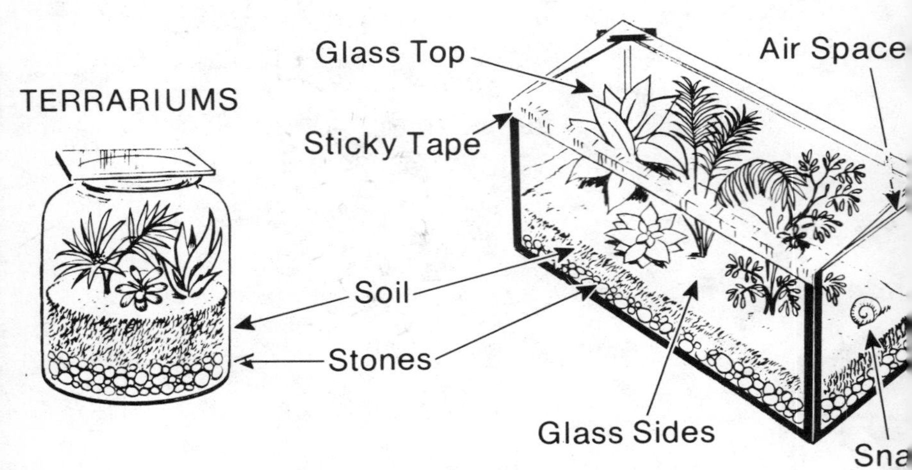

NOTE for Akela: Ivy, moss, and lichens will grow in the glass-covered terrarium that holds heat and moisture.

ARROWHEAD TRAIL Akela's OK Date ______ Recorded by den leader ______

Plant and raise vegetables.

Do this on your own or with your family or den.

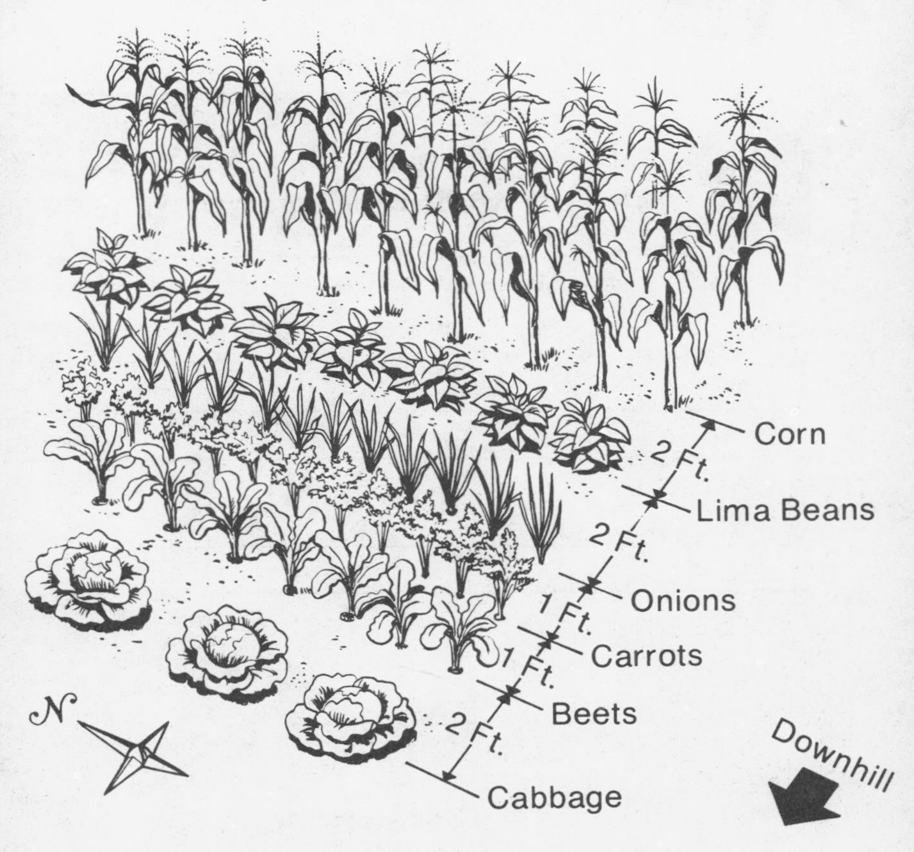

I raised ____

ARROWHEAD TRAIL Akela's OK Date ____________ Recorded by den leader ____________

ELECTIVE

Family Alert

Would you know what to do if your home was hit by tornado, flood, or hurricane? Here are three things you can do.

Talk with your family about what you will do in an emergency.

NOTE for Akela: Guide your son in this project, depending upon your own home, needs, and types of emergencies in your area.

In case of a fire we will ______________________________

____

____

My job is to ____

____

76

ARROWHEAD TRAIL Akela's OK Date ____________ Recorded by den leader ____________

In case of a bad storm or flood, know where you can get safe food and water in your home. Tell how to purify water. Show one way. Know all shut-off places for water, electricity, gas, or oil.

I purified water by ____

____

NOTE for Akela: Boil water for 5 minutes. Ask a health officer for other methods.

We have emergency food and clothing in the

____

____

____

ARROWHEAD TRAIL, Akela's OK Date ____________ Recorded by den leader ____________

Make a list of your first aid supplies, or make a first aid kit. Know where the first aid things will be kept.

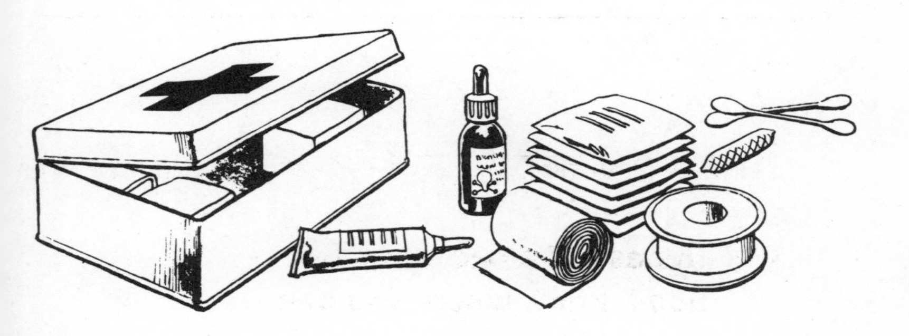

ARROWHEAD TRAIL Akela's OK Date ____________ Recorded by den leader ____________

ELECTIVE

17 Cooking

Cooking is fun, and it is an important job. If you like to cook, you may become a famous chef someday.

Fix your own breakfast. Wash and put away the dishes.

ARROWHEAD TRAIL, Akela's OK Date ______ Recorded by den leader ______

Help fix at least one meal for the family. (Help set the table, cook the food, and wash the dishes.)

I helped to make ________________________

ARROWHEAD TRAIL, Akela's OK Date ______ Recorded by den leader ______

Cook something you haven't cooked before.

I made ______________________________

ARROWHEAD TRAIL, Akela's OK Date ______________ Recorded by den leader ______________

Help to plan, prepare, and cook an outdoor meal.

ARROWHEAD TRAIL, Akela's OK Date ______________ Recorded by den leader ______________

ELECTIVE

18

Outing

A lot of Cub Scouting belongs outdoors with picnics, treasure hunts, and adventure trails.

Help plan and hold a picnic with your family or den.

ARROWHEAD TRAIL Akela's OK Date ________ Recorded by den leader ________

With your folks, help plan and run a family or den outing.

84

ARROWHEAD TRAIL Akela's OK Date ________ Recorded by den leader ________

Help plan and lay out a treasure hunt something like this.

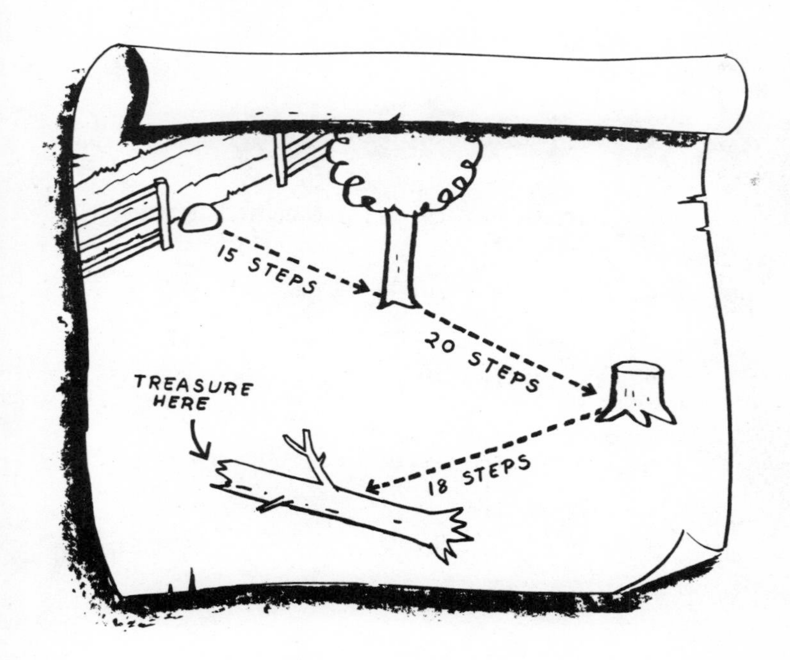

I hid my treasure ______________________________

____

____

ARROWHEAD TRAIL Akela's OK Date ______________ Recorded by den leader ______________

Help plan and lay out an obstacle race. Use this idea or make up your own.

- Jump across an imaginary river.
- Crawl through a cardboard tunnel.
- Jump up and ring a bell.
- Toss a ball into a can.
- Do one forward roll.
- Walk like an elephant for five steps.

This is what I did ______________________________

____

____

______________________ ______________________
ARROWHEAD TRAIL, Akela's OK Date   Recorded by den leader

Help plan and lay out an adventure trail.

In a park or playground set up five games scattered around the park.

1 Guess how many beans are in a jar.

2 Collect as many insects as you can find in 2 minutes.

3 Fold the U.S. Flag.

4 Tie your shoes with your eyes shut.

5 Look for colors, listen for sounds.

My adventures were

____

____

____

____

87

ARROWHEAD TRAIL Akela's OK Date ______ Recorded by den leader ______

Take part in two summertime pack events with your den.

ARROWHEAD TRAIL, Akela's OK Date ______ Recorded by den leader ______

Point out poison plants that grow near your home. Tell what to do if you accidentally touch one of them.

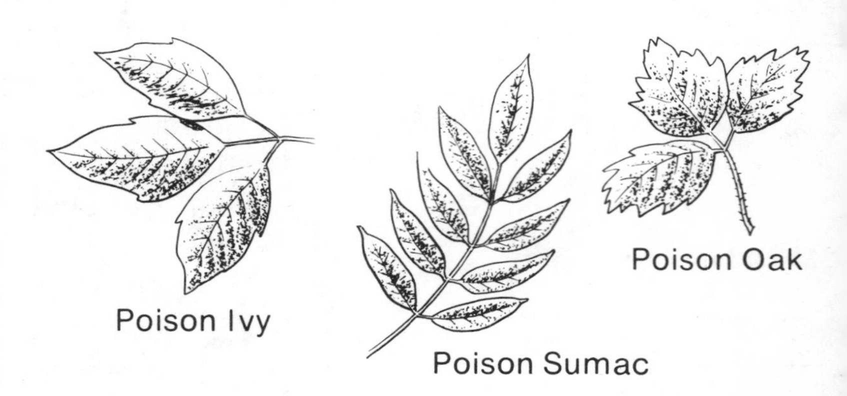

If you touch these plants, wash with soap and water. Then swab with rubbing alcohol.

ARROWHEAD TRAIL Akela's OK Date ______ Recorded by den leader ______

ELECTIVE **19**

Fishing

In fishing, boys and men are equal. The fish does not know whether it's a man or a boy at the other end of the line.

Point out five fish.
Here are some you might see.

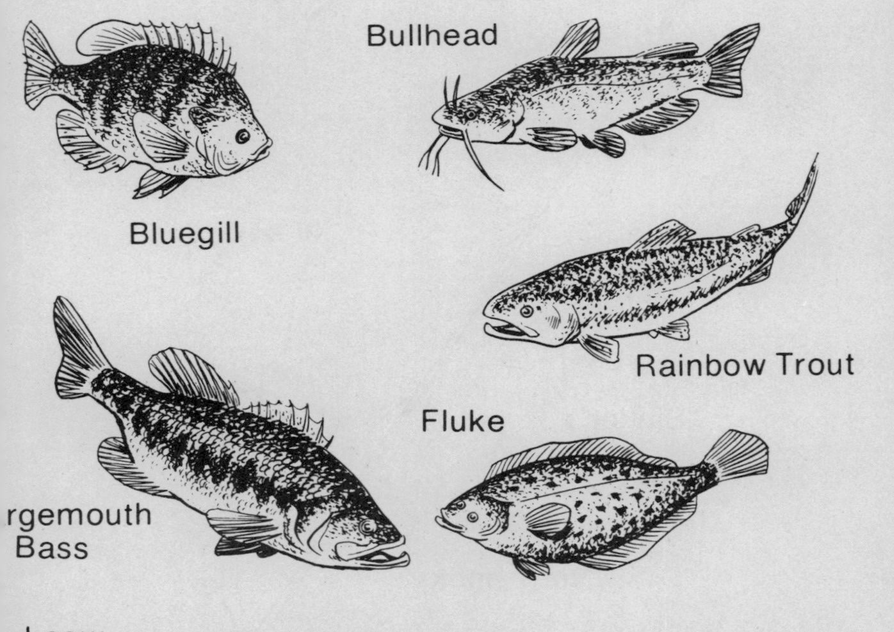

I saw ______________________________

____

ARROWHEAD TRAIL. Akela's OK Date ______ Recorded by den leader ______

Rig a pole with right kind of line. Put on a hook, bobber, and sinker, if you need them. Use it to go fishing.

Line should be no more than half again as long as your pole.

Use 4- to 10-pound test line.

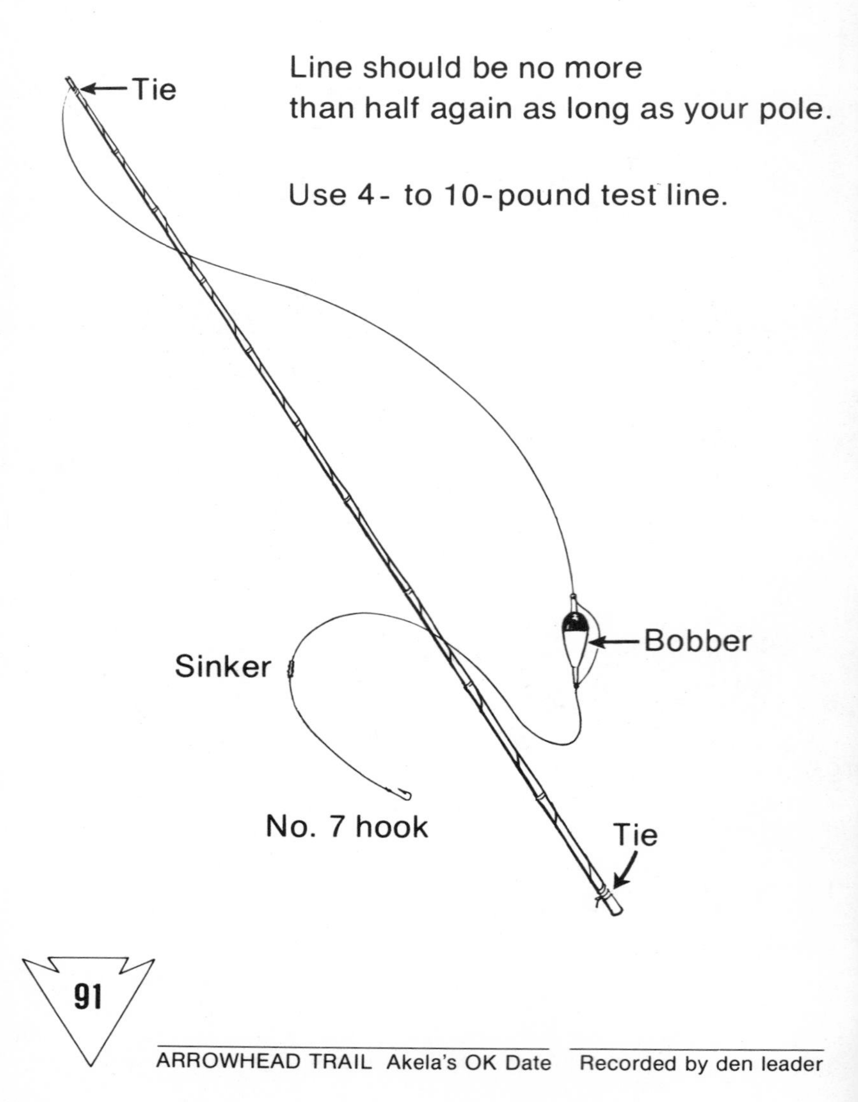

ARROWHEAD TRAIL Akela's OK Date ________ Recorded by den leader ________

Fish with members of your family or a grown-up. Bait your hook and catch a fish.

I caught a ______________________________

92

______________________ ______________________
ARROWHEAD TRAIL, Akela's OK Date   Recorded by den leader

Know the rules of safe fishing.

Be careful of slippery logs and rocks.

That fishhook can catch more than fish. Be careful around other people.

93

______________________ ______________________
ARROWHEAD TRAIL Akela's OK Date   Recorded by den leader

Tell some of the fishing laws where you live.

94

ARROWHEAD TRAIL Akela's OK Date Recorded by den leader

Show how to use a rod and reel.

NOTE to Akela: Cub Scouts should have proper instruction in using rods and reels. Point out safety measures. Adults should go fishing with them.

1 Hold line with finger.

2 Cast rod forward, let up on the line with your finger. When the lure is where you want it, stop the reel by pressing on its edge with a finger.

Lure

Be sure you have plenty of room!

3 Reel in slowly. If you get a strike, play the fish and land it.

4 If you don't get a strike reel in the line and cast again.

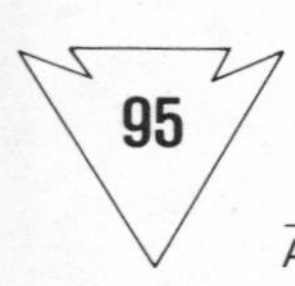

ARROWHEAD TRAIL Akela's OK Date ______ Recorded by den leader ______

ELECTIVE

20 Sports

You may become a superstar or a coach. You can play some sports while you are young, but there are others you can play all your life.

Play a game of tennis, racket ball, or badminton.

NOTE to Akela: Find someone who knows the game to help you.

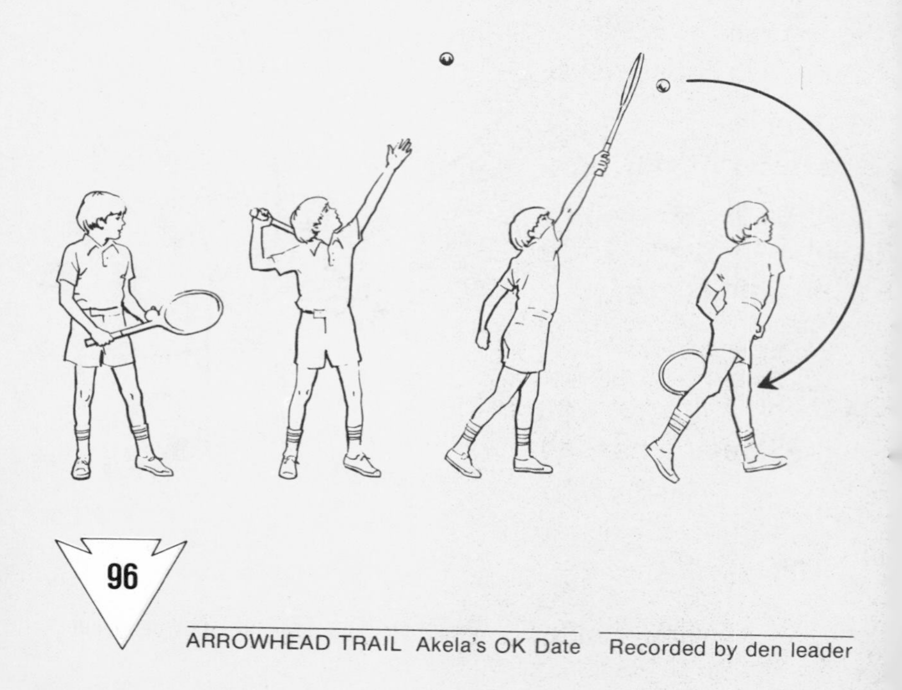

96

ARROWHEAD TRAIL Akela's OK Date ______ Recorded by den leader ______

Know boating safety rules.

Don't overload the boat.
Wear life preservers.

Stay with the boat
even if it leaks.
It will keep you afloat.

When you see lightning or if a storm comes up, head for shore.

ARROWHEAD TRAIL Akela's OK Date Recorded by den leader

Know archery safety rules.
Know how to shoot right.
Put four of six arrows into 1.2-meter target that is 15 steps away from you.

NOTE to Akela: Find an archer who can help you.

ARCHERY SAFETY RULES

- Never put an arrow in your bow until you are ready to shoot.
- Never aim an arrow in the direction of anyone.
- Shoot only where you have a clear view all around you.
- Shoot only where you have a clear view around the target.

ARROWHEAD TRAIL Akela's OK Date ______ Recorded by den leader ______

Know the Skier's Safety Code. Show walking and kick turn. Do climbing with side step or herringbone. Show the snow plow or stem turn, and how to get up from a fall.

NOTE to Akela: Find a skier who can help you.

Wear warm clothes!

SKIER'S SAFETY CODE

- Ski only when properly equipped and clothed.
- Always ski with a buddy.
- Ski under control. Be able to turn and stop.
- Ski on slopes that are not too hard for you.
- Check steepness and snow conditions before you ski.
- Keep fit so that you can ski safely.
- Have good trail manners and respect the rights of others.

ARROWHEAD TRAIL Akela's OK Date ____ Recorded by den leader ____

Know the safety rules for ice skating. Skate without falling as far as you can walk in 50 steps. Come to a stop. Show a turn from forward to backward.

NOTE to Akela: Find a skater who can help you.

ICE SKATING SAFETY RULES

- Always use sharp skates.
- Skate only on safe ice in places where skating is supervised.
- Never skate alone.
- Never skate or walk on thin ice.
- Never throw anything on the ice.
- Never push or grab another skater.

ARROWHEAD TRAIL Akela's OK Date ____ Recorded by den leader ____

In roller skating know the safety rules. From a standing start skate forward as far as you can walk in 50 steps. Come to a stop within 10 walking steps. Skate around a corner one way without coasting. Then do the same coming back. Show a turn from forward to backward.

NOTE to Akela: Find someone who knows the game to help you.

INDOOR SKATING RULES

- Fast skating is not allowed.
- When entering skating floor, give right of way to other skaters.
- In leaving, move slowly to your right. Don't cut across the path of other skaters.
- Do not push or play games that bother other skaters.
- Skate only in the direction of the skating traffic.

OUTDOOR SKATING RULES

- On sidewalks, give walkers the right of way.
- Don't race out of driveways or alleys.
- Avoid skating on rough pavement.
- Don't skate on other people's property without permission.
- Stop and look both ways before you cross a street.
- Obey traffic laws, signs, and signals.
- Don't skate in the street in traffic. Take off your skates and walk.
- Avoid uncontrolled coasting down hills.
- Don't hitch onto bicycles, autos, or trucks.
- Don't skate at night.
- Check equipment before skating. Tighten nuts. Keep straps dry and well oiled. Replace worn straps

ARROWHEAD TRAIL Akela's OK Date ______ Recorded by den leader ______

Show how to make a sprint start in track. Run 45 meters in 11 seconds or less.

(See page 100 for meters.)

Do a 1.2-meter standing long jump.

ARROWHEAD TRAIL. Akela's OK Date ______ Recorded by den leader ______

Play a game of football.

NOTE to Akela: Find someone who knows the game to help you.

Fill in this arrowhead if you have played a game of football or if you are a member of a football league.

ARROWHEAD TRAIL Akela's OK Date ________ Recorded by den leader ________

**Play a game of soccer.
Show how to dribble and kick.
Fill in this arrowhead if you
are a member of a team.**

ARROWHEAD TRAIL Akela's OK Date | Recorded by den leader

**Play a game of baseball or
softball. Fill in this arrowhead
if you are a member of a team.**

ARROWHEAD TRAIL Akela's OK Date | Recorded by den leader

**Show how to shoot, pass,
and dribble a basketball.
Take part in a game.**

ARROWHEAD TRAIL Akela's OK Date | Recorded by den leader

TRAIL SHEET SUMMARIES

Your name: ______________________________ on the

BOBCAT TRAIL

Fill in Seven Bobcat Tracks To Earn the Bobcat Badge

The Cub Scout Promise (1)

The Law of the Pack (2)

The Meaning of Webelos (3)

The Cub Scout Sign (4)

The Cub Scout Handshake (5)

The Cub Scout Motto (6)

The Cub Scout Salute (7)

WOLF TRAIL

Fill in 48 Wolf Tracks To Earn the Wolf Badge

Achievements

1 Feats of Skill (1) (2) (3) (4) (5) (6) (7) (8)

Do one of these three.

2 Flag (9) (10) (11) (12)

3 Keeping Healthy (13) (14) (15) (16)

4 Your Home and Community (17) (18) (19) (20)

5 Tools 21 22 23 24

6 Collections 25

7 Conservation 26 27 28 29 30 31

8 Tying Things 32 33 34 35 36 37

9 Home and Traffic Safety 38 39 40 41 42

10 Family Fun 43 44 45 46

Do two of these four.

11 Religious Activities 47 48 49

12 Using Books 50 51 52

ARROWHEAD TRAIL

Fill in 10 Arrowheads To Earn a Gold Arrow Point
Fill in 10 Additional Arrowheads To Earn EACH Silver Arrow Point

Electives

1 Secret Codes 1 2 3 4 5

2 Dramatics 6 7 8 9 10

NOTE for Akela: Pages 174-76 may be reproduced when more than one boy is using the book.